P9-CML-308

DISCARD

WEST GEORGIA REGIONAL LIBRARY SYSTEM

The Federal Reserve System

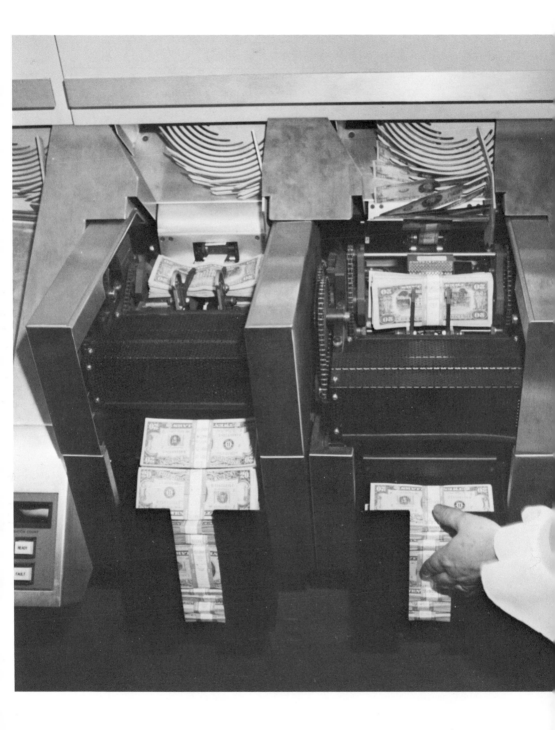

KNOW YOUR GOVERNMENT

The Federal Reserve System

Gary Taylor

CHELSEA HOUSE PUBLISHERS

Cover: *Left:* A worker posts prices at an auction of Treasury bonds.
Right: Interest rates for bank customers.
Frontispiece: A currency-counting machine in a Federal Reserve Bank.

Chelsea House Publishers
Editor-in-Chief: Nancy Toff
Executive Editor: Remmel T. Nunn
Managing Editor: Karyn Gullen Browne
Copy Chief: Juliann Barbato
Picture Editor: Adrian G. Allen
Art Director: Maria Epes
Manufacturing Manager: Gerald Levine

Know Your Government
Senior Editor: Kathy Kuhtz

Staff for THE FEDERAL RESERVE SYSTEM
Assistant Editor: James M. Cornelius
Copy Editor: Phil Koslow
Deputy Copy Chief: Nicole Bowen
Editorial Assistant: Elizabeth Nix
Picture Researcher: Dixon and Turner Research Associates, Inc.
Picture Coordinator: Michèle Brisson
Assistant Art Director: Loraine Machlin
Senior Designer: Noreen M. Lamb
Production Coordinator: Joseph Romano

Copyright © 1989 by Chelsea House Publishers, a division of Main Line Book Co.
All rights reserved. Printed and bound in the United States of America.

First Printing

1   3   5   7   9   8   6   4   2

Library of Congress Cataloging-in-Publication Data

Taylor, Gary, 1947–
    The Federal Reserve System / Gary Taylor.
        p.   cm. — (Know your government)
    Bibliography: p.
    Includes index.
    1. Federal Reserve banks.   2. Board of Governors of the Federal
Reserve System (U.S.)   I. Title.   II. Series: Know your government
(New York, N.Y.)
HG2563.T38   1989
332.1′1′0973—dc 19   88-38178l
                                                                        CIP

ISBN 1-55546-136-0
        0-7910-0896-7 (pbk.)

CONTENTS

427056   WEST GEORGIA REGIONAL LIBRARY SYSTEM

KNOW YOUR GOVERNMENT

THE AMERICAN RED CROSS
THE BUREAU OF INDIAN AFFAIRS
THE CENTRAL INTELLIGENCE AGENCY
THE COMMISSION ON CIVIL RIGHTS
THE DEPARTMENT OF AGRICULTURE
THE DEPARTMENT OF THE AIR FORCE
THE DEPARTMENT OF THE ARMY
THE DEPARTMENT OF COMMERCE
THE DEPARTMENT OF DEFENSE
THE DEPARTMENT OF EDUCATION
THE DEPARTMENT OF ENERGY
THE DEPARTMENT OF HEALTH AND
  HUMAN SERVICES
THE DEPARTMENT OF HOUSING AND
  URBAN DEVELOPMENT
THE DEPARTMENT OF THE INTERIOR
THE DEPARTMENT OF JUSTICE
THE DEPARTMENT OF LABOR
THE DEPARTMENT OF THE NAVY
THE DEPARTMENT OF STATE
THE DEPARTMENT OF TRANSPORTATION
THE DEPARTMENT OF THE TREASURY
THE DRUG ENFORCEMENT
  ADMINISTRATION
THE ENVIRONMENTAL PROTECTION
  AGENCY
THE EQUAL EMPLOYMENT
  OPPORTUNITIES COMMISSION
THE FEDERAL AVIATION
  ADMINISTRATION
THE FEDERAL BUREAU OF
  INVESTIGATION
THE FEDERAL COMMUNICATIONS
  COMMISSION
THE FEDERAL GOVERNMENT:
  HOW IT WORKS
THE FEDERAL RESERVE SYSTEM
THE FEDERAL TRADE COMMISSION

THE FOOD AND DRUG ADMINISTRATION
THE FOREST SERVICE
THE HOUSE OF REPRESENTATIVES
THE IMMIGRATION AND
  NATURALIZATION SERVICE
THE INTERNAL REVENUE SERVICE
THE LIBRARY OF CONGRESS
THE NATIONAL AERONAUTICS AND
  SPACE ADMINISTRATION
THE NATIONAL ARCHIVES AND
  RECORDS ADMINISTRATION
THE NATIONAL FOUNDATION ON
  THE ARTS AND HUMANITIES
THE NATIONAL PARK SERVICE
THE NATIONAL SCIENCE FOUNDATION
THE NUCLEAR REGULATORY COMMISSION
THE PEACE CORPS
THE PRESIDENCY
THE PUBLIC HEALTH SERVICE
THE SECURITIES AND
  EXCHANGE COMMISSION
THE SENATE
THE SMALL BUSINESS
  ADMINISTRATION
THE SMITHSONIAN
THE SUPREME COURT
THE TENNESSEE VALLEY AUTHORITY
THE U.S. ARMS CONTROL AND
  DISARMAMENT AGENCY
THE U.S. COAST GUARD
THE U.S. CONSTITUTION
THE U.S. FISH AND WILDLIFE SERVICE
THE U.S. INFORMATION AGENCY
THE U.S. MARINE CORPS
THE U.S. MINT
THE U.S. POSTAL SERVICE
THE U.S. SECRET SERVICE
THE VETERANS ADMINISTRATION

CHELSEA HOUSE PUBLISHERS

INTRODUCTION

Government: Crises of Confidence

Arthur M. Schlesinger, jr.

From the start, Americans have regarded their government with a mixture of reliance and mistrust. The men who founded the republic did not doubt the indispensability of government. "If men were angels," observed the 51st Federalist Paper, "no government would be necessary." But men are not angels. Because human beings are subject to wicked as well as to noble impulses, government was deemed essential to assure freedom and order.

At the same time, the American revolutionaries knew that government could also become a source of injury and oppression. The men who gathered in Philadelphia in 1787 to write the Constitution therefore had two purposes in mind. They wanted to establish a strong central authority and to limit that central authority's capacity to abuse its power.

To prevent the abuse of power, the Founding Fathers wrote two basic principles into the new Constitution. The principle of federalism divided power between the state governments and the central authority. The principle of the separation of powers subdivided the central authority itself into three branches—the executive, the legislative, and the judiciary—so that "each may be a check on the other." The *Know Your Government* series focuses on the major executive departments and agencies in these branches of the federal government.

The Constitution did not plan the executive branch in any detail. After vesting the executive power in the president, it assumed the existence of "executive departments" without specifying what these departments should be. Congress began defining their functions in 1789 by creating the Departments of State, Treasury, and War. The secretaries in charge of these departments made up President Washington's first cabinet. Congress also provided for a legal officer, and President Washington soon invited the attorney general, as he was called, to attend cabinet meetings. As need required, Congress created more executive departments.

Setting up the cabinet was only the first step in organizing the American state. With almost no guidance from the Constitution, President Washington, seconded by Alexander Hamilton, his brilliant secretary of the treasury, equipped the infant republic with a working administrative structure. The Federalists believed in both executive energy and executive accountability and set high standards for public appointments. The Jeffersonian opposition had less faith in strong government and preferred local government to the central authority. But when Jefferson himself became president in 1801, although he set out to change the direction of policy, he found no reason to alter the framework the Federalists had erected.

By 1801 there were about 3,000 federal civilian employees in a nation of a little more than 5 million people. Growth in territory and population steadily enlarged national responsibilities. Thirty years later, when Jackson was president, there were more than 11,000 government workers in a nation of 13 million. The federal establishment was increasing at a faster rate than the population.

Jackson's presidency brought significant changes in the federal service. He believed that the executive branch contained too many officials who saw their jobs as "species of property" and as "a means of promoting individual interest." Against the idea of a permanent service based on life tenure, Jackson argued for the periodic redistribution of federal offices, contending that this was the democratic way and that official duties could be made "so plain and simple that men of intelligence may readily qualify themselves for their performance." He called this policy rotation-in-office. His opponents called it the spoils system.

In fact, partisan legend exaggerated the extent of Jackson's removals. More than 80 percent of federal officeholders retained their jobs. Jackson discharged no larger a proportion of government workers than Jefferson had done a generation earlier. But the rise in these years of mass political parties gave federal patronage new importance as a means of building the party and of rewarding activists. Jackson's successors were less restrained in the distribu-

8

tion of spoils. As the federal establishment grew—to nearly 40,000 by 1861—the politicization of the public service excited increasing concern.

After the Civil War the spoils system became a major political issue. High-minded men condemned it as the root of all political evil. The spoilsmen, said the British commentator James Bryce, "have distorted and depraved the mechanism of politics." Patronage, by giving jobs to unqualified, incompetent, and dishonest persons, lowered the standards of public service and nourished corrupt political machines. Office-seekers pursued presidents and cabinet secretaries without mercy. "Patronage," said Ulysses S. Grant after his presidency, "is the bane of the presidential office." "Every time I appoint someone to office," said another political leader, "I make a hundred enemies and one ingrate." George William Curtis, the president of the National Civil Service Reform League, summed up the indictment. He said,

> The theory which perverts public trusts into party spoils, making public
> employment dependent upon personal favor and not on proved merit,
> necessarily ruins the self-respect of public employees, destroys the
> function of party in a republic, prostitutes elections into a desperate
> strife for personal profit, and degrades the national character by lower-
> ing the moral tone and standard of the country.

The object of civil service reform was to promote efficiency and honesty in the public service and to bring about the ethical regeneration of public life. Over bitter opposition from politicians, the reformers in 1883 passed the Pendleton Act, establishing a bipartisan Civil Service Commission, competitive examinations, and appointment on merit. The Pendleton Act also gave the president authority to extend by executive order the number of "classified" jobs—that is, jobs subject to the merit system. The act applied initially only to about 14,000 of the more than 100,000 federal positions. But by the end of the 19th century 40 percent of federal jobs had moved into the classified category.

Civil service reform was in part a response to the growing complexity of American life. As society grew more organized and problems more technical, official duties were no longer so plain and simple that any person of intelligence could perform them. In public service, as in other areas, the all-round man was yielding ground to the expert, the amateur to the professional. The excesses of the spoils system thus provoked the counter-ideal of scientific public administration, separate from politics and, as far as possible, insulated against it.

The cult of the expert, however, had its own excesses. The idea that administration could be divorced from policy was an illusion. And in the realm of policy, the expert, however much segregated from partisan politics, can never attain perfect objectivity. He remains the prisoner of his own set of values. It is these values rather than technical expertise that determine fundamental judgments of public policy. To turn over such judgments to experts, moreover, would be to abandon democracy itself; for in a democracy final decisions must be made by the people and their elected representatives. "The business of the expert," the British political scientist Harold Laski rightly said, "is to be on tap and not on top."

Politics, however, were deeply ingrained in American folkways. This meant intermittent tension between the presidential government, elected every four years by the people, and the permanent government, which saw presidents come and go while it went on forever. Sometimes the permanent government knew better than its political masters; sometimes it opposed or sabotaged valuable new initiatives. In the end a strong president with effective cabinet secretaries could make the permanent government responsive to presidential purpose, but it was often an exasperating struggle.

The struggle within the executive branch was less important, however, than the growing impatience with bureaucracy in society as a whole. The 20th century saw a considerable expansion of the federal establishment. The Great Depression and the New Deal led the national government to take on a variety of new responsibilities. The New Deal extended the federal regulatory apparatus. By 1940, in a nation of 130 million people, the number of federal workers for the first time passed the 1 million mark. The Second World War brought federal civilian employment to 3.8 million in 1945. With peace, the federal establishment declined to around 2 million by 1950. Then growth resumed, reaching 2.8 million by the 1980s.

The New Deal years saw rising criticism of "big government" and "bureaucracy." Businessmen resented federal regulation. Conservatives worried about the impact of paternalistic government on individual self-reliance, on community responsibility, and on economic and personal freedom. The nation in effect renewed the old debate between Hamilton and Jefferson in the early republic, although with an ironic exchange of positions. For the Hamiltonian constituency, the "rich and well-born," once the advocate of affirmative government, now condemned government intervention, while the Jeffersonian constituency, the plain people, once the advocate of a weak central government and of states' rights, now favored government intervention.

In the 1980s, with the presidency of Ronald Reagan, the debate has burst out with unusual intensity. According to conservatives, government intervention abridges liberty, stifles enterprise, and is inefficient, wasteful, and arbitrary. It disturbs the harmony of the self-adjusting market and creates worse troubles than it solves. Get government off our backs, according to the popular cliché, and our problems will solve themselves. When government is necessary, let it be at the local level, close to the people. Above all, stop the inexorable growth of the federal government.

In fact, for all the talk about the "swollen" and "bloated" bureaucracy, the federal establishment has not been growing as inexorably as many Americans seem to believe. In 1949, it consisted of 2.1 million people. Thirty years later, while the country had grown by 70 million, the federal force had grown only by 750,000. Federal workers were a smaller percentage of the population in 1985 than they were in 1955—or in 1940. The federal establishment, in short, has not kept pace with population growth. Moreover, national defense and the postal service account for 60 percent of federal employment.

Why then the widespread idea about the remorseless growth of government? It is partly because in the 1960s the national government assumed new and intrusive functions: affirmative action in civil rights, environmental protection, safety and health in the workplace, community organization, legal aid to the poor. Although this enlargement of the federal regulatory role was accompanied by marked growth in the size of government on all levels, the expansion has taken place primarily in state and local government. Whereas the federal force increased by only 27 percent in the 30 years after 1950, the state and local government force increased by an astonishing 212 percent.

Despite the statistics, the conviction flourishes in some minds that the national government is a steadily growing behemoth swallowing up the liberties of the people. The foes of Washington prefer local government, feeling it is closer to the people and therefore allegedly more responsive to popular needs. Obviously there is a great deal to be said for settling local questions locally. But local government is characteristically the government of the locally powerful. Historically, the way the locally powerless have won their human and constitutional rights has often been through appeal to the national government. The national government has vindicated racial justice against local bigotry, defended the Bill of Rights against local vigilantism, and protected natural resources against local greed. It has civilized industry and secured the rights of labor organizations. Had the states' rights creed prevailed, there would perhaps still be slavery in the United States.

The national authority, far from diminishing the individual, has given most Americans more personal dignity and liberty than ever before. The individual freedoms destroyed by the increase in national authority have been in the main the freedom to deny black Americans their rights as citizens; the freedom to put small children to work in mills and immigrants in sweatshops; the freedom to pay starvation wages, require barbarous working hours, and permit squalid working conditions; the freedom to deceive in the sale of goods and securities; the freedom to pollute the environment—all freedoms that, one supposes, a civilized nation can readily do without.

"Statements are made," said President John F. Kennedy in 1963, "labelling the Federal Government an outsider, an intruder, an adversary. . . . The United States Government is not a stranger or not an enemy. It is the people of fifty states joining in a national effort. . . . Only a great national effort by a great people working together can explore the mysteries of space, harvest the products at the bottom of the ocean, and mobilize the human, natural, and material resources of our lands."

So an old debate continues. However, Americans are of two minds. When pollsters ask large, spacious questions—Do you think government has become too involved in your lives? Do you think government should stop regulating business?—a sizable majority opposes big government. But when asked specific questions about the practical work of government—Do you favor social security? unemployment compensation? Medicare? health and safety standards in factories? environmental protection? government guarantee of jobs for everyone seeking employment? price and wage controls when inflation threatens?—a sizable majority approves of intervention.

In general, Americans do not want less government. What they want is more efficient government. They want government to do a better job. For a time in the 1970s, with Vietnam and Watergate, Americans lost confidence in the national government. In 1964, more than three-quarters of those polled had thought the national government could be trusted to do right most of the time. By 1980 only one-quarter was prepared to offer such trust. But by 1984 trust in the federal government to manage national affairs had climbed back to 45 percent.

Bureaucracy is a term of abuse. But it is impossible to run any large organization, whether public or private, without a bureaucracy's division of labor and hierarchy of authority. And we live in a world of large organizations. Without bureaucracy modern society would collapse. The problem is not to abolish bureaucracy, but to make it flexible, efficient, and capable of innovation.

Two hundred years after the drafting of the Constitution, Americans still regard government with a mixture of reliance and mistrust—a good combination. Mistrust is the best way to keep government reliable. Informed criticism

12

is the means of correcting governmental inefficiency, incompetence, and arbitrariness; that is, of best enabling government to play its essential role. For without government, we cannot attain the goals of the Founding Fathers. Without an understanding of government, we cannot have the informed criticism that makes government do the job right. It is the duty of every American citizen to know our government—which is what this series is all about.

Gold ingots in the Federal Reserve Bank of New York. For centuries gold was the basis of money's value, and until the early 1900s most nations' central banks would redeem paper money for its worth in gold. Since the United States went off the gold standard in 1933, the Federal Reserve System has redeemed a note only for a new note.

ONE

The Seal

T he Federal Reserve System was formed by an act of Congress in 1913 to function as a central bank for the United States government and for the public. It also helps regulate the banking industry. In these dual capacities, the Federal Reserve System is among the most powerful institutions in American society. It influences growth of the money supply, affects interest rates, and hence plays a large part in the pace and direction of spending by every citizen and every business. Yet the nature of its operations and the complexity of economic matters such as the money supply make the role of the Federal Reserve a mystery to most Americans.

A first step toward learning the role of the Fed, as it is often called, could be to look at a dollar bill. At the top center of the bill are the words *Federal Reserve Note*. To the left of the portrait of George Washington is a seal in black ink that bears the location of one of the 12 branches of the Fed, such as "Federal Reserve Bank of Atlanta, Georgia"; the letter F, sixth in the alphabet, corresponds to Atlanta's place as hub of the system's sixth district. Above the seal is a guarantee from the government to any person holding the note: "This note is legal tender for all debts, public and private."

These terms hint at the Fed's role as a central bank. In effect, a central bank upholds the value of the government currency and coin by regulating the flow of new money into the economy. It does so chiefly by selling and buying government securities (bonds and other forms of credit) on the open market and by making new loans to depository institutions that need to bolster their reserves. Backed by the government, the Fed thus acts as lender of last resort to the nation's banks.

To support the currency, central banks once kept gold in their vaults. In 1933, however, the U.S. government went off the gold standard, meaning that banks would no longer redeem Federal Reserve notes for their worth in gold to anyone who asked. Gold is still in government vaults, but since 1933 the currency's value has been upheld just as soundly by a promise: that each paper note and metal coin in circulation, its assigned value clearly displayed, is backed by the central bank acting as agent for the government in Washington, D.C. This promise has held fast for more than 50 years, because the United States government is widely considered the most reliable creditor in the world—based on its political stability and on the strength of the economy its citizens have built. The person who spends a dollar is passing the promise from the Fed to the next person.

Before the Federal Reserve was formed in 1913, currency was backed by only limited guarantees. Hundreds of smaller local and state banks issued their own bank notes, promising the holder that the note could be redeemed for gold or as payment of debts. But many of those notes were worth less than face value; most diminished in value as the holder traveled farther from the city or state of issue. If a bank failed altogether, its noteholders had no recourse, often going bankrupt themselves.

Nevertheless, the creation of a central bank chafed against many people's ideas of how the United States was intended to be organized. As ratified in 1789, the Constitution provided for a Congress to set the laws, a court system to ensure that they were obeyed, and an executive branch to direct the nation's

Every Federal Reserve note bears the seal of the Federal Reserve Bank of its origin (New York, in this case) and, above the seal, a promise from the government: "This note is legal tender for all debts, public and private."

16

political affairs; the Bill of Rights, added in 1791, was primarily concerned with civil liberties and religious freedom. At no time did the framers of the Constitution address the highly complex issues of how to furnish a money supply or how to regulate the economy or the banks. (Economic growth was everyone's goal, but it was not thoroughly understood that growth could get out of hand at times and lead to temporary collapse.) Power over the nation's purse strings was originally assigned to the Department of the Treasury, the House of Representatives, and indirectly to the governor of each state. This diffusion of power eventually came to be seen as a weakness, for there was no one body to act as a shock absorber in times of economic crisis or to provide a steady, dependable supply of cash and credit to the merchants and farmers who needed it. By the late 1800s, most city dwellers saw the need for a central bank, and even such rural groups as the Greenback party and the Populist party were critical of the government's policy of tight money, which kept prices for farm goods down. A Populist running for president in 1892 garnered more than 1 million votes. Still, the notion of more currency (either through paper money or silver coinage) met fierce opposition in Congress and among others who believed that eastern bankers would benefit most. The legislation needed to establish a central bank wound a slow course in the face of such disagreement.

To allay fears that a central bank would represent the interests of only one region or industry, the Federal Reserve System was set up to run as something like a cooperative, but not by the government. The system is divided into 12 district banks, each serving as a clearinghouse and source of funds for depositories in its region. Today there are about 5,500 private member banks in the Federal Reserve System, from rural county banks to multinational banks based in New York. (The reserve banks mainly serve depository institutions; they also sell and redeem U.S. savings bonds and Treasury bills for individuals and nonbank firms.) Member banks elect six of the nine directors of their district bank, who in turn recommend some of the people who will sit on two committees in Washington that make or advise on policy for the entire system. The president of the United States appoints the seven members of the system's board of governors, one of whom acts as its chairman for four years. Although only about 40 percent of the private banks in the nation belong to the Federal Reserve System and are its shareholders, this figure does ensure that the interests of agriculture, commerce, and industry are all represented. And although these thousands of member banks are all profit-making ventures, the Federal Reserve System is not: The operating profit it earns by lending money to district banks is returned weekly to the U.S. Treasury.

17

Just as the system is a hybrid of private and public interest, so too does it answer to both spheres, without being controlled by either. Congress can veto its policy decisions on monetary matters but never has; the president cannot command it to set the direction of the economy; the member banks can voice strong disagreement only by withdrawing. The Fed's board of governors, decisively led by its chairman, bases its policy on a combination of the best economic advice its own staff can offer and the advice of the district banks. The board officially answers to congress, but in practice it is guided by the system's one overarching aim: stability in the economy.

Second Most Powerful

The Fed has had only seven chairmen of the board of governors since 1935, when the agency was reorganized along its present lines. Some served in times of crisis, exercising power and making decisions that affected the lives of all Americans. Others served in less troublesome years and worked in the shadows, either striking a less aggressive posture in regulating the economy or accommodating the president's wishes for the direction and pace of growth.

The powers and the role of the Federal Reserve System have evolved since its birth, yet they are still hazy in most people's minds. In 1986, *Newsweek* magazine published a cover story about "the second most powerful man in America," Paul Volcker. Neither his name nor his face were widely familiar, nor was the organization he headed at the time, the Fed. As chairman of the Board of Governors of the Federal Reserve System, Volcker succeeded in squeezing inflation out of America's economy in the early 1980s and earned himself many accolades. He also drew the anger of many people, for his strategy brought about a severe *recession*, a slump in economic activity. It was a matter of opinion whether the recession was worth the price of beating *inflation*, a rise in prices not matched by a rise in worker productivity. In any case, the attention given by the press to the Fed did serve to make people more aware of monetary policy, of the Fed's role, and especially of the enormous power of the board's chairman.

In more normal economic times, few citizens would think of the chairman of the Fed as the second most powerful person in the land. Volcker could not declare war on another nation; he had no power to assemble the armed forces, order Congress into session, initiate legislation, or negotiate with foreign governments. But from 1979 to 1987, he controlled something just as important to daily life. He influenced every American's ability to spend money.

18

In 1986, Newsweek declared that Paul Volcker, chairman of the Federal Reserve Board, held more power than anyone except the president of the United States. As the nation's central bank, the Fed sets monetary policy and thus has much influence over the economy.

IACOCCA: THE POLITICS OF LIBERTY

Newsweek

February 24, 1986 : $2.00

The Second Most Powerful Man in America

A Revealing Profile of Federal Reserve Chairman Paul Volcker

To understand the role of the Fed in American society, one must first see the country as it was without the Fed, in the years before Congress created it. Imagine a world where checks could be written only at stores near a certain bank; a world where those checks might have a different value when used in another city; a world where the value of money could change almost overnight, where a dollar today would be worth only 95 cents tomorrow. Stability was lacking because no private institution was willing or able to guarantee the value of all bank notes in circulation. The seal on every Federal Reserve Note now provides that guarantee.

A machine for sorting and counting currency. Acting as agent of the U.S. Treasury, the Federal Reserve System furnishes currency and coins to banks across the nation through 12 reserve banks.

TWO

Banking and the Creation of Money

Today almost every American is accustomed to using money for virtually all transactions involving goods or services. In truth, money is not indispensable, for a buyer can use a number of other means to make a purchase. Consider the example of a woman who needs a new pair of shoes. She could visit a store and talk to the owner. She could offer to work for the goods by promising to sweep the office; she could barter, trading something she already owns; she could write the merchant a note of her own, promising to pay at a later date. But all these alternatives pose problems.

For one thing, the store may already be clean. Her trade items may not equal the value of the shoes. And her written note offers no reliable guarantee of her ability to pay. To complete the sale the storekeeper and the customer would have to negotiate, and that could take time. Instead, there is now a universally accepted system for this exchange: money. Presentation of two $20 Federal Reserve notes eliminates the need to haggle or barter any further. It also offers security to both sides of the transaction, for both parties accept the Federal Reserve notes to be worth exactly what they claim to be worth. The customer does not need to bargain, and the storekeeper can use the notes to buy more supplies for the store.

In selling the shoes, the merchant and the woman have used a concept often taken for granted in recent times, the concept of money. Simply stated, money is a medium of exchange. But it can be anything that a buyer and seller will accept in making a transaction. Until the Middle Ages, few people needed it, and even today people in some remote parts of the world find it unnecessary. They make their own clothes and grow their own food. Or, they can trade food for the clothes and tools they cannot make themselves. As societies grow more complex and fewer people are able to make everything they need, they use money because its value as a medium of exchange is constant for everyone.

The Origins of Money

More than 4,000 years ago, people in China and in Babylon, the greatest civilizations of their day, used gold and silver as money. Rulers of ancient Turkey used those metals to make the first coins about 600 B.C. The Romans, from about 400 B.C. to 300 A.D., harnessed the power of money in building their empire, issuing coins in lands they conquered and forcing upon much of the ancient world a central coin system. Arabic, Mayan, Indian, and many other societies also used metal coinage.

The portico of the ancient Roman forum, symbol of the Roman Empire's bureaucratic and imperial reach. The empire issued its own coinage in the lands it conquered. One reason the empire fell was the declining value of its money.

Trading moose antlers on the frontier in 1879. In America, salt, animal skins, gunpowder, cattle, and land all served as mediums of exchange when paper money or metal coin was scarce or unavailable.

The first bankers were in fact money changers who profited by selling local coins to travelers from foreign lands. The travelers were willing to pay a little extra to have coins they could use in commerce. The money changers usually owned strongboxes to protect their collection of coins. Local people also found it safer to leave their own funds on deposit with a trustworthy money changer, and thus began a primitive system of banking. As far back as Roman times there have been government regulations regarding the practices of such rudimentary banks.

Specie (coined metal) has not been the only material used for money. Where metals were hard to find, societies have turned to other objects and called them money: whale's teeth, feathers, bark, fur, blankets, tea, gunpowder, or anything that required the owner to perform some specific task of acquisition, such as killing a whale or chopping down a tree.

Modern banking dates to the Banco di Rialto, founded in Venice, Italy, in 1587. Indeed, the word *bank* comes from the Italian word *banco*, or bench—so named because early Italian bankers operated from benches in the street. The Banco di Rialto provided a building for more permanent operations.

Paper notes, or currency, were a natural substitute for specie because they are much lighter. Paper money was probably first employed systematically in China in the 14th century. Paper is just as inherently worthless as metal when not used for its own properties. For example, metal is most useful for making tools, whereas paper is best used for writing on. If a society has an excess of both materials, as China did in the Ming dynasty and the United States does now, the materials can be put to another, symbolic use—as money.

In the 17th century, English goldsmiths began to issue paper receipts to customers who deposited coins in their strongboxes. Those receipts functioned as bank notes, and depositors exchanged them for purchases rather than withdraw their gold from the goldsmith. Although not the first bankers to issue notes, those English goldsmith-bankers are credited with developing the profession to a point where their notes functioned as money. The widespread use of paper money followed in other powerful trading nations of 17th-century Europe—France, the Netherlands, Spain, and the German states. Some of the first bankers in each place started as merchants, amassing enough gold in the course of their trading to set up as moneylenders who issued notes. Each note functioned as a transfer of credit or debt, rather than as a commodity such as gold.

The Creation of Money

By examining the activities of those first bankers, it is possible to understand the process of money creation through the *fractional reserve* method of banking. Under this method, only a portion of a customer's deposit is stored in the vault. The rest is quickly transferred to someone else in the form of a loan. Because the majority of depositors will not be using their money and because those depositors want their money to earn interest, the bank and the depositor are in one sense partners in the business of making loans. In the case of the early bankers, both the depositor who actually owned the gold and the loan recipient who borrowed from the banker holding the gold simply used the receipt, or bank note, for that gold instead of the gold itself. The goldsmiths calculated that if they maintained a fraction of the gold in their vaults—perhaps 15 percent—they would always have enough to meet the few withdrawal demands of their depositors. And as long as all the customers believed their own receipts were worth an amount of gold in the vaults, those receipts could function as money.

As the goldsmiths collected interest on the loans, they would pay a small portion of that back to the depositors in the form of deposit interest. The

A modern bank vault. Banks emerged in the 17th and 18th centuries to store gold for their depositors. They issued receipts that came to be used as money. Today, bank vaults mostly contain paper money, although the Federal Reserve System still holds thousands of gold bars for foreign governments.

deposit interest provided incentive for depositors to leave their gold in the vaults. Meanwhile, each ounce of gold in those vaults came to have the value of two or more ounces: The depositor held one receipt for it, the loan customer held another. As real deposits increased, lending did too. Until someone actually used a goldsmith's receipt to recover the gold, the system would work. In the process, money was actually created. One ounce of gold would create two receipts worth twice its value. The fractional reserve system, therefore, was a tool created to allow bankers to earn more for themselves and for their customers. It is the method used by most commercial banks today.

Some people see danger in such a method, by which loan recipients' debts are actually turned into more money. One peril is a *bank run*, in which depositors lose confidence in the security of their bank and all demand to withdraw the money that has already been loaned to others. Another result of

A bank run, 1868. Before the Fed began issuing currency in 1913, many banks printed their own bank notes, which held value only as long as depositors had confidence in their bank's stability. When confidence waned, frightened depositors raced to withdraw their assets, usually forcing the bank into collapse.

the practice can be inflation, especially if the bank creates too much money by making too many loans in one industry or in one region. But if the banks are prudent, they lend only to people or business firms that stand a good chance of repaying the loan on time and of making new deposits with the proceeds of their activity.

Over the years, the Bank of England (that nation's central bank) inspired the wrath of people who distrusted the fractional reserve method it employed, and some of them challenged the legality of the method. Several English court cases, however, later verified the bank's right to use deposits as loans to other customers. The courts ruled that the deposits are more like loans to the bank than they are money left just for safekeeping. In other words, once a deposit is made it becomes part of the bank's capital.

Fears of inflation and of a bank run are eased today mainly by the Federal Reserve System. Protection from those eventualities and from banking abuses comes from the Federal Deposit Insurance Corporation (FDIC), through which the government guarantees repayment of deposits up to $100,000 per depositor. And through the Federal Reserve System the Federal Reserve Banks serve as "lenders of last resort"—banks that will distribute funds to depository institutions to cover the demands of depositors withdrawing their reserves.

Checks began to replace bank notes as the primary tool of debt transfer in the early 20th century. Each check, like a bank note, represents an inscribed amount of money owed by a bank's customer. A large part of the activity in a modern commercial bank (as opposed to an investment bank or a reserve bank) is to clear the checks, or settle the account, of the person drawing on their deposits. Even checks can be stolen, though, or signatures forged. Since the 1950s, electronic transfer of funds has rapidly become a common means by which banks have conducted the bulk of their business. By using signals recorded on magnetic tape, they have eliminated all need to move a piece of metal or paper from one location to another. Increasingly, individual depositors too can make their payments by electronic transfer. No money is created by the process, but the transfer is simplified.

The Need for Stability

A bank customer's security has improved, then, from the use of gold to the use of elaborately printed bank notes to the use of a cheaply printed check, requiring only his or her signature for validation. Not only have 20th-century banks been spared the expense of printing bank notes—a task now handled entirely by the government—they have also been relieved of the task of convincing the public of the bank note's dependability as an instrument of credit. One large central bank, the Federal Reserve System, by endorsing every bank note in the name of the government, provides that assurance.

Security begets stability, but although money can easily be defined as a medium of exchange, its value may not always be the same. Many factors influence the value of money, some intentional and some beyond human control. The early Romans, for example, in using their system of coins to help build their empire, tried to extend their power artificially by mixing less valuable metals with the gold or silver in the coins. Cheating their citizens, the leaders simultaneously triggered the slow devaluation of Roman coinage, which contributed to the eventual decline and destruction of the empire.

People must have faith in the value of their money. They must also understand that its value sometimes has to change a moderate amount. As the value of a nation's money falls, one result is inflation. A moderate amount of inflation (a range now considered to be between about 2 and 5 percent) can be evidence of a healthy economy, one in which the demand for new products and services just slightly outpaces the current capacity of the factories to supply them. There must also be enough cash and credit in circulation—but not too much—to fund the necessary expansion; and the nation's currency must be accepted by foreign suppliers. Otherwise, consumers revert to bartering one good or service for another, bypassing the monetary system altogether and leaving the nation's output incalculable. This is the case today in many of the world's underdeveloped and socialist nations.

Inflation above the 2 to 5 percent level in a developed nation, or any inflation in a stagnant economy, can lead to financial panic. Such a situation exists when there is more money present—when the government or the central bank has printed more—than is needed to pay for the goods and services that already exist. Inflation can also result from irrational buying or from panic, which allows suppliers to raise their prices unjustifiably fast. The rising popularity of Adolf Hitler and the Nazi party in Germany in the 1920s occurred in part because the German government debased the value of its currency by printing too much in the tumultuous years after World War I. Hitler promised, among other things, to make the money valuable again. More recently, an inflation rate of 934 percent in Brazil in 1988 touched off suggestions that the military would have to replace the civilian government to restore order by some authoritarian means.

In the United States, the highest annual inflation rate since World War II was 13.6 percent, in 1980. The cause was as complex as the economy the rate jump befell. A leap in the price of oil from the Persian Gulf, Federal Reserve policy in the early 1970s, irrationally generous lending by commercial banks, panic speculation in the value of gold, silver, artworks, land, anything thought to be a hedge against monetary inflation—all of these factors contributed. As was proven by the panic buying in commodities, the public's reaction to its fear of inflation can cause even more inflation.

Banks and Central Banks

A bank is a pool of the resources of the many people and companies who choose to entrust their valuables to it. Governments have come to depend on

A Berlin woman lights a fire with worthless currency—"not worth the paper it's printed on"—in 1923. In periods of hyperinflation, such as Germany endured after World War I, confidence in money falters; financial and political upheaval often follow. One purpose of a central bank is to try to prevent such a crisis.

29

The Bank of England, chartered in 1694, was the world's first central bank operating on modern principles. It loaned money to the Crown and provided funds to smaller banks in need. The stability it engendered helped the British Empire to grow.

banks just as individuals do. Especially to raise money for wars, monarchs relied on the largest banks for loans that enabled them to pay and feed soldiers, build ships, and, in the event of military defeat, to pay war damages and reparations. Sometimes governments had to rely on foreign banks when their own nation's banks faltered. The Rothschild banking family of France, for example, came to have enormous influence through its banks around Europe. It acted as an agent of the British government in subsidizing many countries' wars against Napoleon in the early 1800s, and it helped support the Romanov czars in Russia before the Russian Revolution in 1917.

As national governments, both monarchic and republican, grew to be the banks' biggest customers, the utility of a central bank became apparent. William II approved a charter for the Bank of England in 1694, formalizing what had been the bank's unofficial role as lender of last resort to the Crown. By 1850 most of the world's more developed nations had a central bank to print currency, regulate the flow of gold in and out of the country, and generally act as the government's agent in raising funds for its treasury. Perhaps most important, a central bank maintains a supply of reserve funds for use by private banks, thereby adding to small depositors' confidence in their local bank's liquidity.

The notable exception to this pattern was the United States, which for its own peculiar reasons had resisted the trend toward central banking systems. The result of America's dependence on small private banks, though they stood as an emblem of individual freedom from government interference, was sometimes chaotic.

Examples of pre-Revolutionary American money. Some of the colonial governments issued their own money, which often lost value as it was carried to other regions.

THREE

Beginnings

With the ratification of the Constitution in 1789, the 13 colonies now called the United States put aside only some of their internal rivalries. The common alliance of states could not erase the distinctions between Protestants and Catholics, southerners and New Englanders, or farmers and city dwellers. Much organization and reorganization was needed to bring the diverse populace under one economic, political, and legal roof. This effort was complicated by each state's sovereign right to tax goods, collect tariffs, and direct a wide array of governmental operations on its own, without federal interference. The Tenth Amendment to the Constitution set some of the boundaries of federal authority in declaring that "The powers not delegated to the United States . . . are reserved to the States." The Constitution did not provide for a central bank or anything like it, so local control over finances remained a dearly held right.

The internal conflict that ran deepest and that surfaced in each of the 13 colonies was between farmers and city dwellers. This rivalry would influence the nation's money system for more than 100 years until adoption of the Federal Reserve System resolved the dispute. The farmers, who at independence in 1776 made up by far the largest segment of the population, believed the Revolution had been fought to guarantee everyone the opportunity to own land and live as they pleased. They viewed their small, isolated farms as the natural reward of political freedom. For the next 100 years, farmers would

Thomas Jefferson, a proponent of states' rights, wrote that federal control over money and finance would rest on "principles adverse to liberty." A central bank, he believed, would deprive small farmers of some of their independence.

need money mainly at planting and harvesttimes—for buying seed and for paying laborers. Much of the rest of the year, little cash circulated in rural communities, for the residents could provide their own food, clothing, and shelter.

City dwellers, on the other hand, relied mainly on commerce and industry; their need for cash in hand knew no season. Trade with other countries meant growth and prosperity for all, they reasoned, and this required daily exchanges of cash or credit. New banks, owned not by the British but by Americans, were founded to service that need. Like the merchants, the bankers argued that a reliable money system should be the foundation for a modern, industrial economy.

These two groups—farmers and industrialists—divided into America's earliest political parties, the Democrats and the Federalists. Each group had a champion. Thomas Jefferson, a planter from rural Virginia, emerged as a leader of the Democrats and became the nation's first secretary of state. Alexander Hamilton, from New York City, led the Federalists and became the first secretary of the Treasury. Hamilton was determined to promote the rapid

Alexander Hamilton, first secretary of the Treasury, organized the Bank of the United States in part to take over all debts of the individual states. He and Thomas Jefferson frequently clashed on a crucial question: Should power be centralized or dispersed?

commercial growth of the nation. He used his political talents to persuade the first Congress to enact several important pieces of financial legislation.

The First Bank of the United States

Hamilton's most important legacy was his hand in the creation of the First Bank of the United States, founded in 1791 with a charter to operate for 20 years. As a central bank, it can be considered an ancestor of the Federal Reserve System. Not only the largest bank in the young nation, the Bank was also the largest corporation, with headquarters in Philadelphia and branches in several major cities. It employed many people and controlled the finances of many smaller companies, and its leadership enjoyed great power in making decisions. Hamilton and the Federalists considered the bank essential for the growth of business.

Rural Americans came to distrust the central power and wealth of the Bank, viewing it as a dangerous monopoly that threatened sources of credit closer to home. More concretely, they resented any need to borrow money from a large bank far away. In practice, the bank did tend to favor commercial interests in cities along the Eastern seaboard.

Between 1791 and 1811, the only banks in the nation were the Bank and a small number of private firms chartered by state governments. Those smaller banks grew by printing bank notes and issuing them to customers in place of gold or silver for loans. These notes circulated as money in the regions around each bank. At first the smaller state banks were restrained in their production of notes by the Bank. But their importance in local economies increased. When rural interests won a slim majority in Congress in 1811, they killed efforts to renew the central bank's 20-year charter, and it ceased to exist.

By this time, however, some of the Democratic leaders had changed their view of the need for a central bank. James Madison became president in 1809, and, over objections from his party, he argued to retain the bank. The War of 1812 quickly made the bank's absence sorely felt, for without a central bank to control the money system, businessmen created many new state-authorized banks promising easier rules for loans. The war stimulated a need for more loans. Many banks issued their notes without a solid supply of gold or silver to back them up. By the end of the war a financial crisis was under way because those notes had dropped in value.

The federal government also had problems operating without a central bank. It had no safe place to deposit its own funds, no way to move its money, and no method to guarantee the value of its debts. The chaos proved so obvious that even opponents of the First Bank of the United States switched sides and welcomed creation of the Second Bank of the United States in 1816 with another 20-year charter.

The Second Bank of the United States

In their zeal to correct the confusion of the previous five years, political leaders made the second central bank even more powerful than the first, giving it control over a larger supply of the nation's money. Its stock was set at $35 million, four-fifths owned by private investors, one-fifth by the government. The bank was, in effect, a consortium of wealthy investors, and the sympathies of its president, Nicholas Biddle of Philadelphia, lay entirely with the moneyed class.

In 1828 war hero General Andrew Jackson, raised on the frontier, was elected president of the nation. Jackson was suspicious of all banks because of personal experiences with crooked bankers on the frontier. Although the Bank restrained those smaller banks, it still stood as the symbol of the entire banking system, with Biddle at its head. Jackson favored the use of coins instead of bank notes, which could change in value, and disliked the notion of credit. When Congress approved a new charter for the Second Bank of the United States in 1832, Jackson vetoed the legislation.

Things quickly came to a head. The Jackson-Biddle feud was more bitter than the Jefferson-Hamilton disagreement of 25 years before, and the "Bank War" put great strains on the nation's economy. In late 1833, Jackson ordered his Treasury secretary to remove all government deposits from the Bank and to place them in selected state banks. Biddle responded angrily, ordering a halt to all new loans by the Bank and demanding that outstanding loans be repaid immediately. Over the next three years, the nation's economy was squeezed immeasurably by the drying up of new credit, and many businesses failed. Despite the imprudence of Biddle's move, the Bank still held the nation's economy together. In 1836 the Bank's charter expired, and a year later there was a general economic collapse.

In the 27 years after the demise of the Second Bank of the United States, the national economy suffered the uncertainties of a system dominated again by state-chartered banks. More than 1,400 separate banks were issuing their own notes as money. The value of those notes depended on the bank that had written them. Depositors endured violent changes in their money's value, and

This 1834 political cartoon shows Nicholas Biddle (left), director of the Bank of the United States, sparring with President Andrew Jackson (right). In 1836, Jackson refused to renew the bank's charter, a victory for those forces who believed that the central bank benefited only wealthy easterners.

they could not count on banks having reserves enough to cover withdrawal demands.

By 1863, in the midst of the Civil War, Congress was forced to provide relief. It came in the form of the National Banking Act. Essentially, the act created a network of nationally chartered banks, which could legally do business across state lines. More important, it denied state banks the power to issue notes, placing that responsibility solely with the national banks. (The Confederacy continued to rely on money issued by small state banks, weakening the South's economy and hence its war effort.) Without confronting head-on the conflict over central banking, the Civil War banking reforms served as a bridge to the era in which a central banking system—the Fed—could emerge.

Thirty-Seventh Congress of the United States of America:

At the third Session.

Begun and held at the city of Washington, on Monday, the _first_ day of December, one thousand eight hundred and sixty-two.

AN ACT

To provide a national currency, secured by a pledge of United States stocks, and to provide for the circulation and redemption thereof.

Be it enacted by the Senate and House of Representatives of the United States of America in Congress assembled, That there shall be established in the Treasury Department a separate bureau, which shall be charged with the execution of this and all other laws that may be passed by Congress respecting the issue and regulation of a national currency secured by United States bonds. The chief officer of the said bureau shall be denominated the Comptroller of the Currency, and shall be under the general direction of the Secretary of the Treasury. He shall be appointed by the President on the nomination of the Secretary of the Treasury, by and with the advice and consent of the Senate, and shall hold his office for the term of five years unless sooner removed by the President, by and with the advice and consent of the Senate; he shall receive an annual salary of five thousand dollars; he shall have a competent deputy, appointed by the Secretary, whose salary shall be two thousand five hundred dollars, and who shall possess the power and perform the duties attached by law to the office of Comptroller during a vacancy in such office, and during his absence or inability; he shall employ, from time to time, the necessary clerks to discharge such duties as he shall direct, which clerks shall be appointed and classified by the Secretary of the Treasury in the manner now provided by law. Within fifteen days from the time of notice of his appointment, the Comptroller shall take and subscribe the oath of office prescribed by the Constitution and laws of the United States; and he shall give to the United States a bond in the penalty of one hundred thousand dollars, with not less than two responsible freeholders as sureties, to be approved by the Secretary of the Treasury, conditioned for the faithful discharge of the duties of his office; The Deputy Comptroller so appointed shall also take

The National Banking Act, passed by Congress in 1863. The act proposed a national currency and allowed nationally chartered banks to open for business, thus eliminating some of the riskiness of state-chartered banking.

39

Auctioning a $5 gold piece in Virginia, 1864. When small local banks collapsed—or when, as in this case, the Confederacy was losing the Civil War—people sought security in gold.

Changing Times

In the last decades of the 19th century, the farm economy and the industrial economy were moving closer together as technological improvements made them more interdependent. The national banking network could not always keep up with the change of pace. Farmers needed more credit to expand their operations, but most were still dependent on the money supplies of their local banks and could not always get the additional sums needed for growth. Thus, the concept of money supply became an issue in American life.

The term *money supply* refers to the total amount of money in the nation's economy. It includes currency in circulation and bank deposits that can be redeemed on demand. A money supply is considered *elastic* when it can expand to be used as loans, such as to a farmer who wants to buy more land or to a merchant needing another warehouse. When the money supply is inelastic, it curtails growth. Providing an elastic money supply, however, was beyond the powers even of the national banks. Sometimes there was plenty of money to use for growth; at other times the lack of money stalled growth and forced employers to lay off workers. Cycles of boom and bust caused wild gyrations in the levels of jobs, money, goods, and services.

Besides the absence of an elastic currency supply, the network of national banks hampered industrial growth in another way. Money reserves were stored at 50 locations around the nation, and these reserves of money could not be shifted rapidly to regions where withdrawal demands had increased. Immobile reserves added the element of financial panic to the cycles of boom and bust, threatening economic depression with each downturn. Eventually, with the Panic of 1907, Alexander Hamilton's idea of a central banking system found renewed appeal in many influential circles.

The Panic of 1907 began when depositors began demanding their savings from the nation's second and third largest banks. Those banks did not have enough funds to cover the withdrawals. They closed their doors as the fear of lost savings led other bank depositors to seek withdrawals. J. P. Morgan, an

The scene on Wall Street during the Panic of 1907, in which a major bank failed. Banking was becoming more volatile as the Industrial Revolution continued and monopolies emerged. The need for a central bank to stabilize the economy became much more urgent.

J. P. Morgan, the preeminent financier and businessman of his day, about 1910. Morgan's bank calmed the Panic of 1907 by organizing enough loans to save other banks from collapse.

enormously wealthy New York businessman, saved the system by organizing a group of bankers who promised to shift their funds to the banks that were in trouble. Depositors realized they could once again withdraw their savings whenever they wanted. Reassured, they stopped demanding their funds and left them on deposit in their banks. Though the panic ended, bankers and politicians knew the system had come close to collapse. They realized they could not always rely on individuals such as Morgan (who profited hugely from the loans he made). They began to design a new agency that would work like a central bank without the political feuding that had doomed the two banks of the United States in the previous century.

The Aldrich Plan

The issue of a central bank remained politically sensitive, preventing national leaders from moving quickly. With the Aldrich-Vreeland Act of 1908, Congress took a first step by allowing for the emergency issue of new currency in times of financial crisis. The act also provided for the establishment of the National Monetary Commission, which would prepare a major study with recommendations for change in the country's banking and money systems.

As might be expected, the recommendations that emerged, in 1911, formed the center of a new political controversy. Named the Aldrich Plan after the commission's powerful chairman, Senator Nelson W. Aldrich of Rhode Island, the blueprint for reform recommended a central institution to be called the National Reserve Association. This body would set up branch offices in 15 cities around the country but keep all gold reserves in a central repository. It would have power to issue central currency, and it would establish a nationwide interest rate for borrowing money. The plan drew immediate attack from the descendants of those rural interests that had killed the two banks of the United States a century earlier. Led by William Jennings Bryan, a Nebraska populist and a leader of the Democratic party, they challenged the Aldrich Plan, charging that it would place financial control in the hands of a few powerful bankers. With Congress controlled by the Democratic party, the plan was turned aside. It did, however, stimulate debate and demonstrate the need for compromise.

While Woodrow Wilson, a Democrat, campaigned for the presidency in 1912, the chairman of the House Banking and Currency Committee, Arsène P. Pujo of Louisiana, was conducting a congressional investigation of the Panic of 1907. The Pujo hearings presented the nation with a clear picture of the

Senator Nelson Aldrich of Rhode Island initiated legislation for a new government body, the National Reserve Association, to bolster ailing banks in a crisis. The move led to the establishment of the Federal Reserve System.

banking problems: the instability of the money supply, wide-ranging speculation in the stock and commodities markets, unregulated bank activities. Wilson picked up on these themes, and the American public elected him as a president dedicated to financial reform. The nation's economy had matured to a point where its various factions, urban and rural, could reach a compromise that would create the Federal Reserve System. Realizing the need for a central banking system without the awesome and fearful title of a central bank, the new president worked closely with two advisers in drafting a plan for reform. The advisers were Representative Carter Glass of Virginia and H. Parker Willis, a prominent economist. Their plan, called the Glass-Willis proposal, used the framework of the Aldrich Plan as the basic foundation of the Federal Reserve Act. Congress signed the act into law in December 1913.

The Glass-Willis proposal basically sought creation of 20 or more regional reserve banks under private control. This network would perform the nation's central banking functions, including the issue of currency and the storage of reserve funds. Senator Robert Owen of Oklahoma then made several significant changes to the bill. The most important was the appointment of a public supervisory board, to be based in Washington, D.C. President Wilson strongly supported this change, in order to control and coordinate the work of the regional banks. But he wanted this "Federal Reserve Board" to be free of the banker domination that had made the National Reserve Association of the Aldrich Plan unpopular in farming and small-business circles. The Glass-Owen bill provided for such a board to act as a capstone to the system.

Wilson promised that under the Federal Reserve Act banks would be the "instruments, not the masters, of business and of individual enterprise and initiative." By naming William Jennings Bryan as his secretary of state, Wilson placed rural America's loudest spokesman on his own team. He convinced Bryan and other powerful rural leaders that the government would maintain control of the Federal Reserve Board and that the federal reserve notes would be made obligations of the United States, not of private bankers. Creation of the Fed is considered a classic example of presidential leadership. According to

William Jennings Bryan, three times a presidential candidate, in 1896. Bryan spoke for farmers and small-business interests, who were squeezed by the shortage of currency in rural America. They were being "crucified on a cross of gold," he said, meaning that gold, the basis of currency, was mostly controlled by big-city bankers.

Sixty-third Congress of the United States of America;

At the Second Session,

Begun and held at the City of Washington on Monday, the first day of December, one thousand nine hundred and thirteen.

AN ACT

To provide for the establishment of Federal reserve banks, to furnish an elastic currency, to afford means of rediscounting commercial paper, to establish a more effective supervision of banking in the United States, and for other purposes.

Be it enacted by the Senate and House of Representatives of the United States of America in Congress assembled, That the short title of this Act shall be the "Federal Reserve Act."

Wherever the word "bank" is used in this Act, the word shall be held to include State bank, banking association, and trust company, except where national banks or Federal reserve banks are specifically referred to.

The terms "national bank" and "national banking association" used in this Act shall be held to be synonymous and interchangeable. The term "member bank" shall be held to mean any national bank, State bank, or bank or trust company which has become a member of one of the reserve banks created by this Act. The term "board" shall be held to mean Federal Reserve Board; the term "district" shall be held to mean Federal reserve district; the term "reserve bank" shall be held to mean Federal reserve bank.

FEDERAL RESERVE DISTRICTS.

SEC. 2. As soon as practicable, the Secretary of the Treasury, the Secretary of Agriculture and the Comptroller of the Currency, acting as "The Reserve Bank Organization Committee," shall designate not less than eight nor more than twelve cities to be known as Federal reserve cities, and shall divide the continental United States, excluding Alaska, into districts, each district to contain only one of such Federal reserve cities. The determination of said organization committee shall not be subject to review except by the Federal Reserve Board when organized: *Provided*, That the districts shall be apportioned with due regard to the convenience and customary course of business and shall not necessarily be coterminous with any State or States. The districts thus

The first page of the Federal Reserve Act of 1913. By passing it, Congress reined in some of the free-wheeling spirit of enterprise that caused frequent periods of boom and bust. The government, through the Fed, became responsible for regulating the banking industry and for setting a monetary policy that fostered orderly growth.

Arthur S. Link, a Wilson biographer, passage of the Federal Reserve Act ranks as "the greatest single piece of constructive legislation of the Wilson era and one of the most important domestic acts in the nation's history." A 1982 study published by the Federal Reserve Bank of Boston concurred, noting, "With this law, Congress established a central banking system which would enable the world's most powerful industrial nation to manage its money and credit far more effectively than ever before."

As created in 1913, the Federal Reserve System was smaller and less influential than it is now. Over the next three decades, Congress would add to the Fed's powers and responsibilities, positioning it to respond more strongly in periods of growth, crisis, or stagnation.

President Woodrow Wilson in 1914. The previous year he had signed the Federal Reserve Act into law. The system is privately owned (by its member banks) but publicly controlled (by government officials), an arrangement meant to appease many political factions.

FOUR

The Early Years

In its finished form, the Federal Reserve Act of 1913 included several key provisions. Its specific purposes, as stated in the bill's introduction, were "to provide for the establishment of the Federal Reserve Banks, to furnish an elastic currency, to afford means of rediscounting commercial paper, to establish a more effective supervision of banking in the United States, and for other purposes."

The act created a committee to select the locations for the reserve banks. The 12 cities chosen were Boston, New York, Philadelphia, Cleveland, Richmond, Atlanta, Chicago, St. Louis, Minneapolis, Kansas City, Dallas, and San Francisco. Each district bank was represented by one member of its board of directors on a Federal Advisory Board that met four times each year in Washington, D.C. These regional banks were scattered around the nation to provide relief for local banks that might occasionally need to borrow funds from the Federal Reserve System.

The act established a Federal Reserve Board of seven members, including the secretary of the Treasury and the comptroller of the currency. Members were to be appointed by the president, with one member designated as governor and another as vice-governor. The secretary of the Treasury, however, acted as chairman, often placing the Treasury's needs at the forefront. (An eighth member was added in 1922 to give more voice to agricultural interests.) The board's job was to supervise the 12 regional banks.

The first Board of Governors of the Federal Reserve System, 1914. At left is William McAdoo, who as secretary of the Treasury had the most influence on the board. For the first few decades of the Fed's existence, the Treasury's financing needs dominated the system.

The act also gave the board unlimited power to issue currency in the form of Federal Reserve Notes. Those notes would be legal obligations of the United States acceptable as payment for all taxes, customs charges, and other debts. The notes would be redeemable in gold on demand at the Treasury Department of the United States or in gold or lawful currency at any Federal Reserve Bank.

It also allowed every Federal Reserve Bank to establish individual *discount rates* for use in dealing with other banks in each Federal Reserve District. The discount rate is the rate of interest that a private bank must pay to borrow funds from the Federal Reserve System. (The Fed deducts the interest on the loan when it is made, rather than collecting interest at maturity; the interest is thus "discounted" from the original amount of the loan.) Though each Federal Reserve Bank enjoyed the power to set rates based on conditions in each district, the Federal Reserve Board retained the power to approve the rates set by its district banks.

The new system had been designed and approved, but it did not automatically snap into existence. The act designated three government officials to serve as a Reserve Bank Organization Committee. The secretaries of the Treasury and agriculture plus the comptroller of the currency formed this committee and were empowered to implement the new system. They traveled the country to establish the district boundaries and to discuss the system with bankers who would be involved. As with any change in government structure, a transition period was required to allow banks time to adjust to the new rules. The 7,000 national banks were given 60 days to accept the new system. The act provided that they could join the system by purchasing stock, in an amount equal to six percent of their own funds, in their regional reserve bank. In that way, each reserve bank received funds with which to operate, and the local banks received assurance that the system would back them in times of trouble. In many ways, the arrangement was intended to make each reserve bank act like a savings account for the private banks. By February 1914, almost all the firms chartered as national banks had joined. (Many of the state-chartered banks, smaller for the most part than national banks, chose not to enroll in the system.)

The new system required able people in key positions to make it work. By August 1914, President Wilson had selected and Congress had approved the

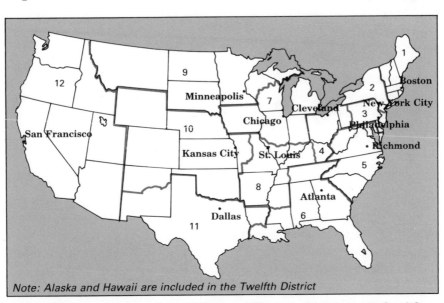

Note: Alaska and Hawaii are included in the Twelfth District

By dividing the country into 12 Federal Reserve Districts, each with a reserve bank, the framers of the system ensured that everyone would have ready access to the central bank's funds.

first Federal Reserve Board. The first board was sworn into office on August 10, 1914. By the end of October, the directors of the 12 regional banks had been chosen. And on November 16, 1914, when the 12 regional banks opened their doors, the federal government immediately apportioned its funds among those 12 locations. The Fed was in business.

The First Leader

When the system opened its doors, World War I was already under way in Europe, creating turmoil on the European as well as the American business scene. Many investors seeking protection from the instability sparked by the war took their gold and cash holdings to the United States. The infusion of these foreign funds caused the American money supply to grow rapidly. In addition, European nations were buying American products in record numbers, and other nations were turning to America to fill a shortage of European-made goods, bringing still more cash into the country. The Federal Reserve System, created in part to assure a sufficient money supply, now faced just the opposite situation: an oversupply of funds.

The duty of tackling the oversupply fell to Benjamin Strong, governor of the Federal Reserve Bank of New York. Scholars regard him as the first important leader of the Fed. Because New York was an international finance and business center, its reserve branch quickly emerged as the key location in the network. Strong had no college education and had lost his first job in the financial industry because of poor handwriting. By 1907, however, he had become an officer at Bankers Trust Company, a large New York bank, and in 1913 became its president. Strong had been one of the industry leaders who persuaded J. P. Morgan to save the banking system in the crisis of 1907. He was the natural selection to head the New York branch of the Fed.

Strong's influence on the Federal Reserve System provides a good example of how an agency grows and changes. Legislation only provides the blueprint. It leaves many questions unanswered. Strong decided on his own to strengthen the U.S. banking system through currency reform. Employing his financial knowledge, he looked for powers within the legislation that would turn the Fed into a dominant agency on banking matters. He realized that the Fed could control the money available to banks merely by purchasing or selling U.S. government securities. It was at this early stage, during World War I, that the

Benjamin Strong unofficially directed the Fed for 20 years from his post as head of the Federal Reserve Bank of New York. He was among the first to see that open-market operations—buying and selling government bonds, through the New York branch—would be the Fed's chief tool for exercising control over monetary affairs.

New York branch under Strong's leadership began one of the most important activities of the Fed: open-market operations.

Open-market operations are the Fed's buying and selling of U.S. government bonds, usually in large quantities, to alter the money supply. Securities dealers in the private sector—the open market—are on the other side of these transactions. The fact that the buying and selling occurs on the open market allows free economic forces to determine the securities' price and interest rate. The Fed has two other tools for this job, but open-market operations emerged as the most important. It remains the most frequently used method today, and the New York bank remains the headquarters for carrying out this operation. Its open-market office is known as the Desk.

Today the decision to change the size of the money supply through open-market operations is made by the system's 12-member Federal Open Market Committee (FOMC). If the Fed wants to limit the money supply, it simply increases its sales of government bonds. As bond traders write checks for their bond purchases, the Fed deducts the amounts from the reserves of the banks involved, and their reserves grow smaller. The banks then have less reserve capital to lend. If the Fed instead wants to increase the money supply, it starts buying more U.S. government securities. This time the bank accounts of the bond traders grow larger as they deposit checks from the Fed for the bond purchases. The reserves in the banks increase, and they have more money to lend.

The Federal Reserve Act had authorized the system to perform open-market operations. But it did not authorize the existence of the FOMC that today supervises those operations. The history of this committee is one example of the way the system changed and grew in response to real needs, without specific legislation to make it work. In 1922, Strong invited the leaders of the five eastern Reserve Banks to join an unofficial committee that would meet to make decisions about the purchase of government securities. However, the members of the Federal Reserve Board in Washington, D.C., saw that committee as a threat to their power because it could meet outside their supervision. But they recognized the need for an authority to supervise open-market operations. So they quickly dissolved Strong's committee, then reappointed its members to a new committee operating under board supervision. The new committee was entitled the Open Market Investment Committee, forerunner of the FOMC that supervises open-market operations today. It was formally recognized by statute in 1933 and 1935.

Reorganization in the 1930s

The early leadership of Strong demonstrated the power of open-market operations and made the Fed a powerful agency during those hectic years between World War I and the Great Depression of the early 1930s. But Strong's death in 1928 left a leadership vacuum in the system. And the crisis of the Great Depression proved so severe that new legislation was needed to increase the Fed's powers. The depression began after stock prices collapsed in October 1929. Although that stock market crash ranked as only one factor creating the Great Depression, it started a chain of events that led directly to changes at the Fed. Because many stock buyers had purchased stocks on credit, they had to use cash reserves to pay their brokers when those stocks lost their value. The need for cash put pressure on the banks. The Fed was unable to move fast enough to increase the money supply. Banks and companies began to fail; people lost their life's savings, and perhaps 25 percent of the workforce lost their jobs. In this environment of despair, Congress and President Franklin D. Roosevelt, who had been elected in 1932, acted to make the Fed more responsive.

The changes occurred after a congressional investigation of national banking practices in 1933. The investigation exposed several significant banking problems and prompted Congress to approve two important acts reforming the Federal Reserve Act of 1913. Those measures were the Glass-Steagall Act of 1933 and the Banking Act of 1935. In general they placed more power in the hands of the Federal Reserve Board in Washington, D.C.

The Glass-Steagall Act created the Federal Deposit Insurance Corporation (FDIC) to insure bank deposits. With accounts insured, the public could have faith in the banking system again. Even if the bank failed their money would be refunded by the insurance fund. The act also separated commercial banks from a practice called investment banking, in which bankers act as brokers or agents to solicit funds for new and unproven companies. Investment bankers buy securities from a new company, providing that company with money to launch its operations. They also provide funds for mergers and acquisitions in a similar fashion. Investment banking activities involve much more risk than normal banking functions, so the Glass-Steagall Act sought to protect depositors by

A breadline in Chicago, 1930. The stock market crash of 1929 and the ensuing depression demonstrated that the Federal Reserve System, as originally set up, did not have sufficient regulatory powers to fend off such economic calamity.

President Franklin D. Roosevelt signs the Banking Act of 1935; at far right is Fed chairman Marriner S. Eccles. The act strengthened the Federal Reserve System and its ability to safeguard bank customers' deposits.

requiring commercial banks to sell off or close their investment banking divisions.

The Banking Act of 1935 changed the Federal Reserve Board structure. It also marked the emergence of another important leader for the system: Marriner S. Eccles. He was the 13th son of a Mormon Scottish immigrant who had 2 wives and 21 children. Although his father was a millionaire who controlled many companies, Eccles began working at the age of eight. He became a successful businessman, assistant secretary of the Treasury, and a member of the Federal Reserve Board. An important adviser to President Franklin Roosevelt, he favored large-scale government spending programs as a way to stimulate the economy. Congress sought his help in 1934 as it investigated ways to rescue the nation's banking system. Eccles believed major changes in the Federal Reserve System were warranted, and he agreed to serve as chairman of the board if President Roosevelt would agree to support those changes. Roosevelt did, and Eccles's plan became the Banking Act of 1935. He became chairman in 1934, holding the position for 14 years.

President Roosevelt dedicates the new Federal Reserve Board building in Washington, 1937. Previously housed in the Treasury's offices, the Fed became both symbolically and actually more independent of the Treasury during the Roosevelt years.

The act of 1935 also centralized the open-market operations that had been used to adjust the money supply. Although the FOMC was organized in 1933, each of the 12 privately run Federal Reserve Banks still had the authority to buy or sell government securities independently of the committee recommendations. Eccles wanted to centralize that function by giving the FOMC full control over open-market operations throughout the nation. He also wanted the Fed to control the appointment of the 12 Federal Reserve Bank governors, no longer allowing the individual bank boards to select their own. The Banking Act of 1935 accomplished Eccles's goal of making the Federal Reserve Board the central authority for nationwide banking through several specific reforms. The act

- Reorganized the Federal Reserve Board, changing its name to Board of Governors of the Federal Reserve System, adding a seat, and eliminating the seats held by the secretary of the Treasury and the comptroller of the currency. Membership thus fell from eight to seven. All seven would be appointedby the president, who would also appoint a chairman to serve a four-year term.

- Transferred executive authority at the Federal Reserve Banks from individually selected chairmen to the governor appointed by the Fed at each location.

- Reorganized the FOMC, which had consisted of the 12 Federal Reserve Bank governors. Instead, it created a committee composed of the 7 board members plus representatives from 5 of the 12 banks.

- Authorized the board of governors to change reserve requirements for member banks (the money they must keep on reserve at their Federal Reserve Bank) without declaration of an emergency.

- Required the Federal Reserve Banks to establish the discount rate every 14 days with approval of the board of governors.

Although those changes helped to stabilize the banking system, too many worldwide factors were keeping production down. The Great Depression did not end until World War II forced growth upon the nation's factories and businesses as they expanded to provide the materials demanded by the war effort. During this period the Fed found itself in competition with another branch of the government, the U.S. Treasury. The Treasury wanted to keep interest rates low so it could manage the debts from the war without high interest costs. But the Fed believed interest rates should rise to keep individual spending and prices low. Eccles believed the money supply had to be

President Harry S. Truman (center) at a press briefing on the 1952
federal budget. The Truman era (1945–52) was marked by close coop-
eration between the Fed and the Treasury as the United States recov-
ered from World War II. In 1951, however, an accord signed by the
two agencies gave the Fed complete freedom to set interest rates as it
saw fit.

reduced at the end of the war, or the nation would face another dangerous
enemy—inflation. By 1951 the dispute had reached a point where President
Harry Truman had to intervene. He sided with the Fed and ordered the
Treasury to recognize that monetary policy would be set by the Fed. Once
again the Fed had increased its power without the need for new legislation.

During the next 20 years the Fed was able to operate with little resistance
from the public or private sectors. Technological advances created the need for
new companies and economic expansion. As the economy grew naturally, it
seemed to manage itself. By the late 1970s, however, the challenge of inflation
was threatening the nation's economy and the time had come for a new
direction in policy. Once again a strong chairman would rise to lead the Fed in
a time of crisis.

Paul Volcker, chairman of the Fed from 1979 to 1987, delivers one of the agency's semiannual reports to Congress in 1982.

FIVE

A Revolution at the Fed

Saturdays are often silent in the nation's capital, as policymakers leave the public arena for the suburbs. But Saturday, October 6, 1979, will long be remembered as an exception to the norm. On that day the Federal Reserve System announced a change in the direction of its policy, a shift that shook the financial world. By launching what some have called a war on inflation, the Fed reoriented its institutional philosophy; the mechanism for carrying out the philosophy therefore also had to change. The new philosophy was *monetarism*, and it proved to be the main weapon for stemming inflation in the 1980s. With this strong-arm tactic, the Fed cemented its position at the center of America's economy. Paul A. Volcker, the chairman of the board of governors, led the revolution, and in the process became both hero and villain.

Monetarism is the theory that control of the money supply should be the key strategy in stabilizing an economy. When on October 6, 1979, Volcker ordered banks to increase the amount of money they held in reserve on some types of funds, he was trying to stabilize the economy through monetarist means. With more of their funds locked in reserve, the banks had less money available for loans. Because they could not make as many loans, they could not create as much new money. In slowing the creation of money by banks, Volcker was not adding to the powers of the Fed. He was simply using a strategy granted the Fed by Congress but untested by previous chairmen. They had never had to use the tactic because inflation had never grown to become the serious problem it was in the 1970s.

The Old Policy

Until 1979, the Fed as the central bank had employed two other strategies to influence money creation. As Benjamin Strong discovered in the system's formative years, the Fed could limit or encourage bank loans through open-market operations, buying or selling government bonds to affect the reserves available to commercial banks. Beginning in the 1930s, the Fed used its power over interest rates more often, as a second strategy for economic control. The federal government wanted to alleviate the economic crisis of that decade by spending money itself. With large public works projects such as the construction of parks, dams, and roads, the government could stimulate the economy and put people to work, encouraging them to put more of their own money into circulation.

To spend money, however, the government first had to borrow it, like anyone else. It therefore wanted interest rates to be low. By centralizing power in the Board of Governors of the Federal Reserve in Washington, D.C., the Banking Act of 1935 had in effect created a triumvirate of economic policymakers—the president, the secretary of the Treasury, and now the chairman of the Fed, Marriner Eccles. To cooperate with the government's recovery plans, Eccles let the Federal Reserve accept a passenger-seat role in this triumvirate, allowing President Roosevelt and Secretary of the Treasury Henry Morgenthau jointly to take the wheel in guiding monetary policy. The Fed continued to establish interest rates and conduct its open-market operations in ways that would help the government through the depression. By cooperating with the executive branch, Eccles put the entire Federal Reserve System at the disposal of the nation's best interests, something the 12 district presidents might not have been able to do in a time of crisis. When Eccles finished his third term in early 1948, the chairman of the Federal Reserve Bank of Philadelphia, Thomas B. McCabe, was nominated to succeed him.

After the outbreak of the Korean War in June 1950, wholesale prices leapt 16 percent in 8 months, promising serious inflation to consumers if the Fed did not begin to act independently of the Treasury and raise its discount rate. The Treasury Department had long insisted on keeping its regular bond interest rate at 2½ percent, an artificially low mark that allowed the government to continue borrowing cheaply. But the rate also made government bonds rapidly lose their attractiveness to large investors because most other municipal and corporate bonds were paying a much higher rate. The Fed, holding its accustomed course, acceded to the Treasury's wishes.

A public works sewer project in San Diego, 1941. From the 1930s to the 1970s the government and the Fed based economic policy on the Keynesian approach, which holds that government spending stimulates the national economy.

On January 31, 1951, President Truman made the unprecedented (and still never repeated) move of calling the entire 12-member Federal Open Market Committee to the White House. Something had to be done, he urged, "to maintain confidence in the Government's credit and in Government securities." The Fed, as the Treasury's agent, was obliged to support the Treasury's financing efforts in the market, but the government's needs (to borrow cheaply) were not always the same as the nation's needs (to avoid inflation). The upshot of the meeting was mixed, but it is possible that McCabe's resignation just four weeks later signaled an imminent shift in Fed policy. Truman appointed William McChesney Martin, Jr., formerly the assistant secretary of the Treasury, to take the reins at the Fed.

Newly Independent

Shortly before Martin's arrival, the Fed was set free from the Treasury's influence. By the Treasury-Federal Reserve Accord of 1951, the Fed was given leave to make monetary policy without consulting other agencies or

William McChesney Martin, Jr., left, and President Lyndon B. Johnson, in 1965. Martin served as chairman of the Fed from 1951 to 1970, guiding the economy along a steady course toward low inflation and low interest rates.

persons. Though the president would periodically suggest some desired economic goals, the Fed had more autonomy. The arrangement worked. With the exception of minor recessions after the Korean War and in 1959, economic growth went unabated in the next two decades. A very able financial administrator, Martin steered a middle course between accommodating the Treasury's borrowing needs and dampening any threat of inflation. In the economically stable years of Martin's tenure from 1951 to 1970, interest rates stayed low, inflation seemed a forgotten word, and the demand for funds made by member banks upon the reserve banks clipped along at a regular and manageable pace.

The catchphrase Martin used to describe the Fed's policy—"leaning against the wind"—is a useful metaphor to explain how the Fed generally tries to counteract trends in the market. When inflationary pressures build, the Fed raises interest rates and takes money out of the reserves; when a slump or slowdown threatens, the Fed releases more money into circulation.

In the 1970s, however, inflationary pressure on the U.S. economy increased dangerously. The executive and legislative branches of the government proved unable to solve the crisis. The stage was being set for the Fed to emerge in

1979 as the nation's primary economic manager, with monetarism as its primary tool.

President Nixon took what proved to be a futile first step to slow inflation by imposing a series of controls and freezes on wages, prices, and rents in August 1971; they lasted through late 1973. The scheme could only delay the inevitable, however, as prices and wages shot up to account for lost time as each phase of the program ended.

A more serious round in the inflationary spiral began in October 1973 when the Arab nations, for political reasons, quadrupled oil prices and placed an embargo on oil shipments to the United States. The resulting shortage of oil and gasoline forced the price of energy higher throughout the world, which in turn meant higher prices for just about everything else, because energy is required for manufacturing. As prices rose for consumer goods, workers throughout the economy demanded higher wages. Employers, in turn, raised prices again so they could afford to meet the demands of the workers. This sequence recurred continually during the 1970s, despite official efforts to halt the spiral. Later in the decade, Congress proposed additional taxes on oil and oil companies to dampen demand. Both Nixon's price freeze and congressional pressure were aimed at the symptoms of the price rise rather than its cause, however. Inflation was still the nation's primary problem.

As prices rose, Americans borrowed at a feverish pace to pay bills and, if they could, invest in commodities whose prices were also skyrocketing—gold, silver, art, real estate. As the cost of everyday purchased goods increased, the value of American money declined because more money was required to buy those goods. By loaning Americans the money needed to live, the banking system was creating more money. Too much money was chasing too few goods, and the further creation of money itself caused further inflation. By 1979, the average price for purchased goods was increasing annually at a rate of 13.3 percent. (This means that an average American had to pay 13.3 percent more for the same goods and services at the end of the year than at the start.)

Most economists consider a small amount of inflation—the one to three percent annual rise that had been common since World War II—to be a healthy sign of economic growth. But in the 1970s everyone agreed that the annual inflation rate of six to eight percent meant that the economy was out of control. Nevertheless, politicians were reluctant to let the Fed take strong steps—raising interest rates—to prevent money growth. When interest rates increase, businesses cannot as easily borrow to expand. They cannot afford to keep all their employees, and workers are laid off. And when unemployment increases, voters blame their elected officials. Presidents and members of

Congress therefore usually fear the Fed's efforts to slow the growth of the money supply more than they fear inflation.

Sometimes politicians may even favor inflationary conditions. Indeed, many political and economic observers have long believed that a president will enjoin the Federal Reserve to slightly increase the money supply in the months before an election. With such an increase, and without triggering a serious round of inflation, the economy can take on a rosier look, giving citizens more pocket money and thus promoting a sense of economic prosperity. The incumbent politicians thereby stand a better chance of reelection. In the decades when the Fed's main tool of control was interest rates, this argument was difficult to prove, possibly because the scheme was not sure to work even if it were tried. Since the 1970s, however, as the principles of monetarism began to work their way into the Fed's regular vocabulary, such preelection fine-tuning has become more likely. For example, before the November 1972 presidential contest between President Richard Nixon and Democratic nominee George McGovern, the nation's money supply rose a startling average of 11 percent over a 5-month span; the figure had been 3 or 4 percent before. Fed

Motorists lining up for gas, New Jersey, 1974. The Arab oil embargo of 1973 sent the price of oil skyrocketing, touching off general price inflation and wide unemployment. As a result, the value of the dollar began to slip.

Arthur Burns, chairman of the Fed from 1970 to 1978, bore the brunt of the inflation shock of the 1970s. The Fed tried to devise new ways of combating the wild swings in interest rates, money supply, and prices but was largely unsuccessful.

chairman Arthur Burns (1970–78), a Nixon appointee, may well have been enjoined by the incumbent president to follow this immoderate course.

For that and other reasons, inflation began to get out of hand. Only the Fed was in a position to do something forceful: It could raise the discount rate it charged to member banks and thereby slow their lending practices. Political desires for low interest rates had to give way, and under Burns's successor, G. William Miller (1978–79), they did. But by the time of Miller's tenure a climate of near-panic had taken hold in the nation. A second oil-price shock in 1979, coupled with the takeover of the U.S. embassy in Teheran by Iranian revolutionaries, had disastrous effects on the nation's economy and on its self-confidence. When Miller resigned to become secretary of the Treasury, President Jimmy Carter appointed Paul Volcker to head the Fed.

Volcker was known to favor a different, more stringent approach to price instability. Monetary policy since the 1930s had been based on the premise that manipulating the government's budget was the best way to stimulate growth—spending more, for example, to fend off a slump. Now the president would hand over that task to the Federal Reserve, and let it try to direct the economy not through budgets but through manipulation of the money supply.

Volcker Steps In

At the time of his appointment, Volcker was serving as president of the Federal Reserve Bank of New York, the second most important job in the Federal Reserve System. He was in a natural position to move up a rung to the top job. Moreover, his ideas on monetary philosophy seemed to be worth trying at that juncture. It should be noted that restricting the growth of the money supply to

President Jimmy Carter (left) looks on as his nominee, Paul Volcker, is sworn in as Fed chairman, 1979. Volcker forewarned the president that the drastic steps needed to halt inflation would hurt Carter politically, but Carter appointed him anyway.

slow inflation was not an idea that originated with Volcker. The theory of monetarism was given its first elaboration in the 1960s by economists Milton Friedman and Anna Schwartz. But Volcker had the ability to put the theory into practice, and he did so during his stint at the helm from 1979 to 1987. He had warned Carter that he would tighten money growth if appointed chairman of the Federal Reserve Board. He later said he was surprised when Carter appointed him anyway, just a year before the elections; but Carter was apparently more concerned with the economy's health than with his own chances for winning reelection.

In contrast to former chairmen, Volcker was determined to make the Fed a more assertive force in the economy. He had concluded that monetarism should have a major role in the fight against inflation. He also championed the concept of an independent and active Federal Reserve Board, one that would base decisions on the needs of the national economy rather than the fears of the politicians. Volcker demonstrated the Fed's newfound determination immediately. On October 6, 1979, without even informing the president first, he announced the Fed's new ways of operating: It would restrain the money supply, not raise interest rates, to bring down inflation. And it would require some banks to put an additional eight percent of their funds into the local Federal Reserve Bank, where they earn no interest. Banks would have that much less to lend, and the money supply would shrink. Some observers thought the policy was sure to spark a recession. A year later the Fed tightened money still further even though President Carter was at that moment fighting for reelection against challenger Ronald Reagan. With Reagan's victory, Volcker gained even more opportunity to make the Fed a central force in the national economy. The Reagan administration set out in 1981 with a well-publicized bias against government management of the economy and society. It promised to reduce government, reduce taxes, and reduce regulation. The result was a gap in economic leadership that Volcker was able and willing to fill.

Volcker's resolve was destined to make him a center of controversy because his efforts to tighten credit brought much pain. As the Fed successively raised the discount rate through the district reserve banks to record levels, the cost of funds to member banks went up in tandem. Banks passed on that cost to their customers. The nation's largest commercial banks, called money-center banks and mostly based in New York (Citicorp, Morgan Guaranty, Chase Manhattan, and a half dozen others), will set their *prime rate* of interest to reflect shifts in the Fed's discount rate, and most smaller banks quickly follow suit. The prime rate is what banks charge their most creditworthy customers,

Redirecting the Fed: Paul Volcker

The Federal Reserve System has often been closely identified with its leader, who is in a position to influence the opinions—or at least the votes—of the board of governors' six other members. Under Paul Volcker, who served as chairman of the Federal Reserve Board from August 1979 to August 1987, the leader's role became still more important. There was no official change in the board's makeup in Volcker's era. Instead, his tools were forcefulness and a sound grasp of the technicalities of monetary policy. He took over at a time when inflation had been souring the American economy for almost a decade, and he proceeded to lead a successful campaign against it.

Son of the city manager of Teaneck, New Jersey, who wanted him to be an engineer, Volcker opted instead to study economics at Princeton University. He achieved an A average and played on the basketball team as well. Because of a generous financial aid program, he then chose to tackle graduate work at Harvard University's school of public administration instead of entering its law school. He completed the coursework for a Ph.D. but never wrote his dissertation because he won a fellowship to study at the London School of Economics. In the 1950s and 1960s he held a number of important financial positions at banks and in government, becoming an under secretary in the Department of the Treasury in 1971. His reputation brought him appointment in 1975 as president of the Federal Reserve Bank of New York. When President Jimmy Carter needed someone to head the Fed four years later, Volcker's name topped the list.

Despite Volcker's eminence as an economist, some aspects of his personality contrasted with the usual image of a banker. He dressed without much care, smoked cheap cigars, and lived in a small, cluttered apartment. His sense of humor won friends among the press—he once attended a costume party dressed as the Jolly Green Giant (he is six feet, seven inches tall), paying mock homage to his nickname. He enjoyed joking about his profession, once telling reporters that bankers are like the Puritans—"They have a haunting fear that someone, somewhere, may be happy."

If necessary, Volcker could keep his critics off-balance. When meeting with advisers or politicians, he mainly listened, saying little himself. But when pressed, especially by someone comparatively unlearned in the intricacies of economic theory, he could go on at length with a baffling array of statistics, causes, and effects, leaving his listener bewildered. Indeed, he was devoted to his mission, having been raised to value personal sacrifice and public service. He lightheartedly complains of his first experience with monetary restraint—trying to survive in college on a monthly allowance of $25 from his parents. (As chairman of

Volcker tells the House Banking Committee in 1985 that "gross imbalances" plague the U.S. economy and that the Fed alone cannot solve them. The Fed moved into the national spotlight during his tenure as management of the economy became more complex.

the Fed he first earned $57,000 a year, perhaps one-fifth of what he could have made on Wall Street.)

Volcker redirected the Fed's operations shortly after taking the helm. Since the 1930s the system had exerted control over monetary policy mainly by adjusting interest rates. In October 1979, struggling to halt inflation, he announced that the Fed's chief tool would henceforth be control of the money supply. Targeting the expansion of credit—the pool from which individuals and corporations borrow—by requiring banks to keep larger reserves, Volcker thrust the Fed more fully into the core of the country's financial machine. He did not adopt a wholehearted faith in monetarism, as some economists did. Rather, he used some principles of monetarist thinking to take the drastic steps needed to end a crisis. It worked: By 1986, inflation had fallen from more than 13 percent to about 1 percent annually.

The criticism Volcker drew for the Fed's belt-tightening moves in the early 1980s was also directed at the Fed itself, for he guided it to such a lofty and influential place in the government that some thought he was interested in power. Little else about him supports that charge. The Fed was created to function as a central bank, and Volcker skillfully made it do just that, for the betterment of the nation. He once said of the Fed, "We are caught in the position of sometimes reminding people of [economic] limits." He continues to be recognized as one of America's leading authorities on monetary affairs.

71

with smaller, riskier concerns, as well as consumers, having to pay a still higher rate. The prime rate usually stands about two to four percentage points higher than the discount rate, and it is the prime rate that generally determines the level of economic activity and ultimately affects the average citizen.

Weathering the Recession

At one point in December 1980 the prime rate exploded to 21½ percent—its highest level ever. The hardest-hit industry was housing, and with families simply unable to afford a mortgage at rates that high, new construction virtually stopped. Auto loans were also prohibitively high, and Detroit, as the hub of auto manufacturing, suffered enormously. Unemployment in housing and heavy industries exploded, with the nationwide rate reaching 10.8 percent around Christmas 1982. That mark rounded out a year of misery for millions of Americans. The nation's gross national product, the total output of goods and services, actually declined by about five percent in that year, its worst showing since the 1930s.

Despite high unemployment and the recession created by tight money policies, Volcker went largely unchallenged. He exercised more control over the economy than could have been envisioned by the legislators who established the Federal Reserve System in 1913. One factor alone may explain why the politicians let Volcker act unchecked: His tactic of monetarist stringency was succeeding. To the commercial bankers who form the bulk of the Fed's forum of critics and fans, no price was too high for the protection of their assets against inflation.

However, the new tack was not an immediate and unalloyed success— interest rates bounced from 8 to 18 percent in the early 1980s, and national output was jerked up and down like a sidecar. Many leading economists were not convinced that the Fed's monetarist experiment was the best course. On the other hand, Milton Friedman, dean of monetarist thinkers, goaded the Fed along. His position was that a regular annual expansion of the money supply by three to four percent would lead the economy toward steady growth. In fact, Volcker recognized that the monetarists' theoretical world, the one of Friedman's ideas, provided only part of the answer. The overall economy cannot and would not respond in lockstep to every shift in the money supply. Other factors come into play, including business cycles, political events, and human psychology—an investor's confidence and a consumer's needs are often impossible to predict. Nevertheless, by limiting new credit so the money

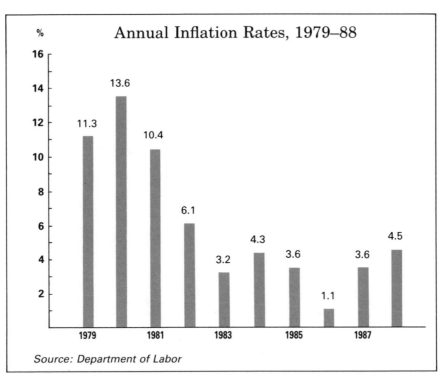

Annual Inflation Rates, 1979–88

%

16

14 — 13.6

12 — 11.3

10.4

10

8

6 — 6.1

4.3

4 — 3.2   3.6   3.6   4.5

2 — 1.1

1979   1981   1983   1985   1987

Source: Department of Labor

By raising interest rates sharply and slowing the growth of the money supply, the Fed touched off the recession of 1981–82. In defeating inflation, however, the Fed readied the economy for strong economic growth over the rest of the decade.

supply would not rise or fall precipitously, the Fed helped to rein in one cause of inflation. In the real world, it worked: The inflation rate dropped from 13.3 percent in 1979 to 1.1 percent in 1986. Prices stabilized, and reasonable economic growth returned to the American economy.

With that success came a new direction for the Fed. The growth of the agency's power seemed to be a result of its chairman's leadership. Volcker could persuade the board of governors and leading politicians of the course he wanted to pursue; no previous chairman had been so effective. Just as important, the revolution in the Fed's philosophy, from rate watching to monetarism, and the revolution in the way it accomplished the desired stability—inducing a painful recession in order to root out inflation—marked another step in the agency's transformation. The Federal Reserve had become far more visible, and perhaps more powerful, than ever before.

The Eccles Building, the Fed's headquarters, on Constitution Avenue in Washington, D.C. The policy-making groups—the board of governors, the Federal Open Market Committee, and the Federal Advisory Council—meet here to set interest rates and adjust targets for the money supply.

SIX

Structure and Operations

The structure of the Federal Reserve System, like several other institutions of the U.S. government, arose from a compromise between different factions in American life and different social beliefs. As a result, it fits into no simple category of government, which raises some questions about control. Does the Fed answer to either Congress or the president? Officially it answers to Congress, but it operates autonomously. Can its decisions be challenged? They can, but rarely are effectively. To what branch of government does the Fed belong: executive, legislative, or judicial? To none: It is an independent, nonprofit, regulatory agency. The board of governors must submit several annual reports to Congress, including a review of its operations, and special reports twice each year explaining the state of the economy. Despite this legislative supervision, however, there is little Congress would do to reorganize the system's affairs and powers without consulting the board itself for a solution.

So the Federal Reserve System occupies an unusual position in American government. Its power clearly goes well beyond what had been envisioned by the politicians who created it in 1913. Moreover, opponents of its policies and decisions have little recourse. Once the president appoints economists to the

Fed's board of governors, there is no way to remove those individuals before the end of their term unless they commit crimes or exhibit extremely bad judgment in their official duties. With its oversight of the banking system, the Fed has become the dominant power in the nation's economy. Many have criticized its maneuvers and called for its abolition, but as long as the Fed succeeds in its role it is doubtful that any organized opposition will become strong enough to topple it.

Today the Fed has several specific operational goals. Its long-range goals are to guarantee that growth in money and credit will be sufficient to encourage growth in the economy and that prices will be reasonably stable. Promoting stable prices means ensuring a stable dollar, but one that also responds to trends, meaningful fluctuations, and shifts in power in the international monetary markets. The relative strength of the dollar against other currencies affects the nation's balance of trade with those other countries. Another long-range goal is the health and stability of the American banking industry. By overseeing banking operations (approving or blocking mergers, regulating lending practices and capital reserves), the Fed can help create an atmosphere that inspires the confidence of consumers. A short-range goal that serves this end is to prevent financial panic by acting as the lender of last resort for banks in trouble. Another short-range goal is to initiate policies to fight inflation or deflation (a decline in the price of goods or services, which can also be harmful).

The Governors and Their Advisers

Although it has demonstrated its power as an independent arm of government, the Fed does not function without regard for the rest of the government, especially its elected officials. The chairman of the Fed meets regularly with presidential advisers and congressional leaders to explain policy decisions and listen to political concerns. As only one of seven members of the board of governors, the chairman cannot make policy alone. In reality, however, the chairman is usually a persuasive leader who can convince other board members to vote a certain way. A majority vote of four to three is sufficient to pass any motion or policy. Board members are appointed by the president and confirmed by the U.S. Senate for terms of 14 years. (Except for lifetime judgeships and for the 15-year term of the comptroller general of the United States, who directs the General Accounting Office, an arm of Congress, this 14-year term is the longest of any post in the federal government.) The chairman and vice

President Ronald Reagan (left) and Fed chairman Paul Volcker at the White House, 1983. Volcker met frequently with Reagan to apprise him of the Fed's new anti-inflationary policies.

chairman are named by the president for four-year terms from among the board members, and their designations must also be approved by the Senate.

Though most opinion about policy flows eventually to the Federal Reserve headquarters in Washington, it does not all originate there. Groups to advise the board of governors exist on many levels, each providing information about regional conditions. One body established by law is the Federal Advisory Council. It is composed of 1 prominent banker from each of the 12 districts; each district board of governors selects them to confer with the national board quarterly on the state of business, credit, and finance around the nation. Rotating membership allows for a variety of opinion to work its way up to the governors. Nonstatutory or informal bodies also serve as consultants to the board, including the Chairmen's Conference (composed of the chairmen of all 12 Federal Reserve Banks) and the Presidents' Conference (composed of the 12 presidents). Both groups meet periodically to discuss policy and make recommendations. The Presidents' Conference, mostly concerned with coordinating the entire system's regular operations, also advises the Federal Open Market Committee.

Some Functions of the
Federal Reserve System

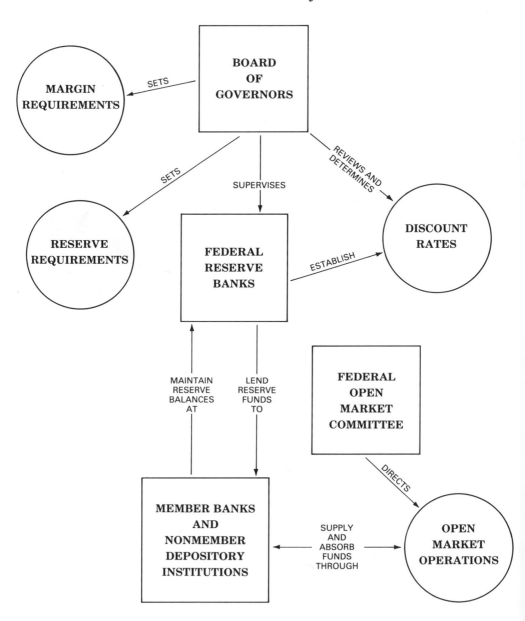

Still other perspectives are given by the Consumer Advisory Council, a body also established by statute. Among its 30 members are representatives of the financial industry, a variety of its consumers, and academic and legal experts on consumer affairs.

After Congress passed the Monetary Control Act of 1980, another board was set up, the Thrift Institutions Advisory Council. It voices the concerns of savings banks, savings and loan associations, and credit unions, all of which were put at a disadvantage by the 1980 act's deregulation of the banking industry. Many of these smaller institutions have folded or been absorbed by larger banks since the early 1980s. A central element of the 1980 act directed the Fed to make reserve funds available to all depository institutions, not just member banks.

Regulation and Oversight

The prime function of the board of governors is to formulate the nation's monetary policy, but it fulfills other duties, too. One is to supervise and regulate member banks and banking companies all over the country. In this capacity, for example, it has authorized 45 private firms, as of early 1989, to be primary dealers in Treasury bond auctions. These firms, mostly large banks and brokerage houses, must participate substantially in the Treasury's weekly sale of bonds to finance the federal government.

A smaller though increasingly important task of the Fed is to regulate the American branches of foreign banks. Under the International Banking Act of 1978, the board of governors has authority to impose reserve requirements and some lending policies on these banks, which control a growing share of America's credit pool. The Fed gives these banks access to its services and closely supervises their transactions with Federal Reserve banks.

The Fed also establishes and administers regulations designed to protect bank customers. In this capacity, one of its recurrent tasks is to conduct a regular review of every depository institution's reserves. The largest banks, for example, must submit a weekly report to examiners from their Federal Reserve district to prove that the bank has enough hard reserves, or liquidity, to continue operating. From 1913 until 1980, banks were required to hold as liquid reserves a minimum of 16¼ percent of certain deposits; in 1980, Congress reduced the reserve requirement for most banks to 12 percent, thereby freeing more of each bank's deposits for loans to the private sector.

In this area, banks regulate themselves for the most part, borrowing daily from the other banks (they pay what is called the *interbank rate*, also called the Fed Funds rate, on these loans) to maintain their liquidity at 12 percent. If its creditworthiness is in doubt—if it has made too many loans that stand a poor chance of being repaid—and no other bank will lend to it, the member bank can go to the discount window at its Federal Reserve Bank for a short-term loan. The reserve bank charges the borrowing bank interest on the loan, based on the discount rate each reserve bank sets for its region. The discount rate is usually slightly lower than the interbank rate, but a bank in need of funds will usually go to the Federal Reserve System only when it is in trouble. Since 1980, small depository institutions and other nonmember banks can go to the window if they lack access to funds on the open market. Generally, though, the Fed discourages banks from coming to the discount window for short-term cash needs: Borrowing of that sort unnecessarily alters the total supply of money. Banks' short-term needs can usually be filled from the pool of credit already in circulation.

The Fed oversees the operations of the network of 12 Federal Reserve Banks, reviewing each bank's budget and approving the appointments of president and vice-president at each of the banks. Each reserve bank has its own board of directors to oversee individual operations. These boards establish the discount rates to be charged to other banks who borrow money from the system, and these rates must be approved by the board in Washington, D.C. Profit is not the directors' motive when setting the discount rate—the stock of each Federal Reserve Bank is owned by its member banks, but they do not control operations. For a fee, the reserve banks help member and nonmember banks clear checks and electronically transfer funds. As agents of the U.S. Treasury, the reserve banks provide currency and coins to banks as needed. There are branches of the 12 district banks established in 25 additional cities.

Federal Open Market Committee

The Federal Open Market Committee (FOMC) is a third executive division of the Federal Reserve System. Its membership includes the seven members of the board of governors, the president of the Federal Reserve Bank of New York, and four other reserve bank presidents who serve one year each on a rotating basis. Traditionally, the FOMC selects the Fed chairman to be its

The trading room for open-market operations at the Federal Reserve Bank of New York. The Fed's two main valves for controlling the flow of the money supply are open-market trading and the discount rate. Interest rates in the 1980s had to stay comparatively high, in part because of large federal budget deficits.

chairman too, with the president of the New York bank as vice-chairman. According to statute, the FOMC decides whether the Federal Reserve System will buy or sell U.S. government bonds, an activity that enables the system to influence the amount of money available to banks for loans. These transactions are the open-market operations that are the Fed's chief tool for influencing the nation's money supply. Each year the FOMC establishes a schedule for meetings to conduct open-market operations. In the 1980s, the committee gathered as often as eight times per year. The topics of its meetings are held in strict secrecy, to prevent market speculators from betting their hunches before any policy shifts are made public the next day.

Setting Monetary Policy

All daily operations of the Fed are conducted in accordance with its most significant function: the establishment of monetary policy. Not to be confused with monetarism, monetary policy includes all actions by the Fed that affect financial and credit conditions. (Monetarism is the philosophy that money supply holds the key to a stable economy.) By influencing the amount of money available to banks for loans, the Fed can influence the creation of money and the speed of growth in the economy. It has three tools at its disposal for influencing money available to banks.

Open-market operations remain its primary tool because they provide a way for the Fed to intervene directly in financial markets. When the Fed decides more money is needed in the economy, it orders the Federal Reserve Bank of New York to buy back large amounts of U.S. government securities. That, in turn, places checks from the Fed into the bond sellers' bank accounts, providing them with more funds to lend throughout the economy. When the Fed senses that money should be tightened, it instructs the New York reserve bank to sell government securities, and that activity pulls money out of the economy as buyers send their checks to the Fed.

The discount rate serves as a secondary tool. By raising or lowering the interest rate on funds borrowed by banks, the Fed can influence the decisions of those banks to borrow. When the rate is high, banks will borrow less and have less money available for loans. When the rate is low, those banks will borrow more and, in turn, make more loans.

Third is manipulation of reserve requirements, which may rank as the Fed's most powerful tool for adjusting the money supply. By this rule, each institution must keep a certain small percentage of its deposits in reserve at its district's reserve bank or as vault cash. The Fed can raise reserve requirements by ordering member banks to place more of their funds in reserve. This maneuver limits the funds each bank has available for loans and, thus, for money creation. When it lowers reserve requirements, the Fed frees up more funds for each bank's use in lending. This is the Fed's most powerful tool because it forces member banks to limit their lending. Open-market operations and manipulation of discount rates merely influence those banks by increasing the *cost* of money. If those banks wish to borrow at higher rates, they can. With a change in reserve requirements, however, the Fed has affected the *supply* of money, leaving member banks no choice but to change the amounts they have on reserve.

82

It was the use of all three tools together plus adoption of a new method for setting money supply goals that caused such a shock on October 6, 1979, when Chairman Volcker moved to combat inflation. The Fed raised the discount rate 1 percent, from 11 to 12, and raised the reserve requirements. By wielding its power over both the cost and the supply of money, the Fed sent a signal to the financial markets that it was serious about controlling the reserve base.

Measures of Money Supply

The real revolution was the announcement of a change in the Fed's method for controlling the money supply. That change involved a new focus on bank reserves rather than interest rates. As a result, interest rates could rise or fall to any point at which borrowers could be found. Meanwhile, the Fed would set targets for the economy's total supply of money and use its powers to meet those goals.

In setting its targets for money supply, the Fed analyzes a number of factors. Money supply, or the total stock of cash and credit in the economy, can be divided into several parts for the Fed to examine. When it detects a change in any of those parts, it can use its various tools to bring them back into line with the desired goals. The basic money-supply segment is called M1 and is the narrowest gauge of the measures. M1 is the aggregate of all currency in circulation, all demand deposits at banks (usually meaning checking accounts), all Negotiable Order of Withdrawal (NOW) (checking accounts that pay interest) and Automatic Transfer Service (ATS) accounts, and smaller items such as travelers checks. In 1979 the M1 total was about $362 billion, of which about $120 billion, or one-third, was currency and coin in circulation. This M1 segment was enough to support a gross national product of $2.4 trillion.

Other M figures more closely gauge the size of the working money supply. M2 is a more encompassing measure than M1, taking in the figure for M1 plus such big-number items as savings accounts, money market mutual fund holdings, and the funds (called Eurodollars) held by American corporations through their overseas offices. The Fed calculates a few more M figures, each more inclusive than the last, but in analyzing the economy's needs, M2 and M3 play the most important role. These segments, sometimes called the *monetary aggregates*, reflect most directly what the average consumer is doing with his or her money in a given month. An interesting sidelight to the Fed's task of measuring the nation's money supply is that each April the M1 segment can

Fed chairman Alan Greenspan gestures to President Reagan in a 1988 meeting of economic officials in the White House; to the right of Reagan is Treasury secretary James Baker. Though the Fed's governors usually consult with congressional and administration officials before making major policy changes, neither branch can dictate to the Fed.

take a wild leap, up or down depending on tax laws, as people pay their income taxes or get refund checks. A smaller fluctuation often occurs in December, as Christmas shopping picks up pace. In the agricultural parts of the country, money supply still wavers at planting time and harvesttime, just as it did in the 18th and 19th centuries.

Besides monitoring the money supply, the Fed also reviews a broad measure of debt in the economy. Staffs of economists in New York and Washington prepare projections about needs in the economy. They consider a number of events and factors, anything that might provide a clue to future trends. One example might be a large increase in the number of new housing permits issued, indicating that construction is picking up and that aspiring home buyers will be taking out mortgages in the near future. The board and the FOMC respond to such signs of life (or quietude) in the economy by formulating the maneuvers they will need to keep money creation in line with the target for growth. A bureaucracy as large as the Federal Reserve System faces a double-edged challenge: It must be all-seeing, if it is to regulate the ballooning industry of banking; and it must move quickly in response to the dynamic force of world credit and monetary markets. Creating the right amount of money and targeting a realistic level of growth each year requires a highly sensitive and creative hand. The challenges for the future are many.

On October 19, 1987, traders at the New York Stock Exchange look on in disbelief as the Dow-Jones average crashes more than 500 points. With markets becoming more volatile, the Fed struggles to blunt the shocks and to ensure that financial institutions remain sound.

SEVEN

The Fed's Future

In September 1985 the treasury secretaries and finance ministers of the world's five largest industrial nations held a series of meetings at the Plaza Hotel in New York City. This group, called the Group of Five, decided that the value of the U.S. dollar in relation to the other major currencies was too high. The group therefore decided that for the good of all they must coordinate their nations' monetary policies to bring the dollar more into line with America's actual service and manufacturing presence in the world economy. In other words, the dollar's value should be lower because the world was less interested in buying American goods. The mechanism for such an enormous revaluation would of course be each nation's central bank, with as much cooperation from the commercial banks as could be mustered by political means. James Baker, U.S. secretary of the Treasury, and Paul Volcker, chairman of the Fed, took leading roles in formulating the pact.

So France, Great Britain, Japan, the United States, and West Germany set forth to bring about the goals of what came to be called the Plaza Agreement. The value of the dollar immediately fell almost five percent against the Japanese yen and the West German mark, the two currencies that have progressively inched up on the dollar ever since as leaders of the monetary pack. The U.S.

Some members of the Group of Five (the leading industrial nations) at the Plaza Hotel in New York City, October 1985; Paul Volcker is second from left. The world's central banks, led by the Federal Reserve, orchestrated a fall in the dollar's value to bring it more into line with America's declining industrial potency.

Treasury asked the Federal Reserve System to begin buying marks and yen on the international market and to let other nations' central banks sell dollars. (The Federal Open Market Committee directs the level of this activity, and the Federal Reserve Bank of New York carries out the transactions.) This plan would bring down the dollar's relative value. The goal was to make U.S. goods more affordable on foreign markets by lowering the value of the dollars they were denominated in. The United States's large foreign-trade deficit would thereby come down. By early 1989, the plan had worked to an encouraging degree. The dollar slipped from its 1985 peak of about 240 yen to 122 yen. The yearly trade deficit (the gap between the value of goods exported and those imported) dropped from about $160 billion in 1987 to $125 billion in 1988.

One consequence of such a major revaluation would usually have been to bring about a round of inflation at home. As U.S. goods became cheaper abroad, imported goods would simultaneously become more expensive, and

American consumers would have to pay more for everything from Italian leather to Japanese cars to German electronics. But inflation stayed down, in the three to five percent range. Why? There were several factors involved, but one was that the Fed's management of the money supply at home was a stabilizing force. Money growth kept pace with real gains, based on productivity, in the purchasing power of American households and businesses.

The shift has not been without cost in the United States. Japanese industry was enabled to virtually take over whole markets with its more powerful currency, chiefly in the production of some computer parts and electronic goods. Its corporations began buying American land and companies at a record rate, and in the middle and late 1980s its securities firms bought about one-quarter of the Treasury bonds sold each year because U.S. firms no longer had the resources to fund the federal government's deficits. Some of this problem was attributable to political concerns: The Reagan administration continued to mismanage its fiscal policy, relying on Japanese firms to finance the deficit instead of cutting its own spending or raising taxes. Monetary policy, as carried out by the Fed, steered a straight course, keeping the value of the dollar steady and not letting it fall too low against the yen or the mark.

The Passing of Monetarism

The Fed's experiment with monetarism in the early 1980s is generally viewed as a success. Paul Volcker set out to bring down inflation, and he succeeded.

The principal threat to the economy is still inflation, but other conditions have changed. A growing consensus in Congress, among economists, and, most important, among the public, believes that the government must do something to bandage the wounds left by the recession of the early 1980s and the foreign takeovers of U.S. companies that ensued. If it does intervene more directly in the economy, the administration of President George Bush will be returning, in modified form, to the monetary-fiscal theory of government spending called *Keynesianism*. Reliance on monetarism for guiding monetary policy could slowly ebb. Named for the British economist John Maynard Keynes, who died in 1946, Keynesian theory dictates that governments can manipulate their budgets to influence social and economic conditions, as Franklin Roosevelt's New Deal programs of the 1930s did so effectively. The government can inject money into selected sectors of the economy to alter the overall distribution of wealth. Society changes as the government shifts its attention from one sector to the next.

The economic collapse of the 1930s was far more serious than the problems the American economy faces in the late 1980s and early 1990s. Parts of the banking industry, however, are in great need of help. The Federal Deposit Insurance Corporation (FDIC), a not-for-profit agency created during the Great Depression to reassure bank customers of their deposits' safety, has seen its funds slowly drop as it helps failing banks. The most notable of these is the Continental Illinois Bank, once the nation's seventh largest commercial bank, which required a bailout in 1984. A parallel agency, the Federal Savings and Loan Insurance Corporation (FSLIC), has had to come to the aid of so many floundering savings and loan institutions that in 1986 it plummeted into negative net worth. The FSLIC, not to mention the hundreds of savings and loans still asking for emergency funds, will require tens of billions of dollars from the government in order to return to solvency.

Steelworkers in Pennsylvania march on Labor Day, 1982. Millions of Americans were pinched by the Fed's anti-inflation policies during the recession of 1982–83, when interest rates hit 20 percent and unemployment reached 11 percent. Home mortgages became too expensive for many people.

Manufacturing industries are also asking the government for protection. Shoes made in Taiwan or Korea are threatening the livelihood of American shoemakers; the textile, rubber, steel, and automobile industries have asked the federal government to shield their products from competing imported goods. All told, the federal government is being asked to intervene in the marketplace on an unprecedented scale. As the United States is a democracy, the government cannot ignore all of the requests. The Reagan administration was quite firm in its opposition to protectionist moves as a general practice. It was generous, however, in bailing out individual corporate giants, including Continental Illinois, Lockheed, and Chrysler. The main counterforce to such government generosity is, of course, the size of the national debt. Under the Reagan administration, the debt almost tripled in just 8 years, to nearly $2.6 trillion. In 1988 alone the interest on the debt was about $150 billion, almost 15 percent of the federal budget. Paul Volcker, speaking before Congress in late 1988 as an elder statesman on economic matters, warned that if the government's annual deficit does not come down substantially, inflation is likely to rise, and eventually America's economy as well as its national security could be irreparably damaged. The U.S. government is, therefore, asked both to bolster large segments of the economy *and* to cut its spending.

What this means for the Federal Reserve System is difficult to assess. Chairman Alan Greenspan, appointed by President Reagan in 1987, has quietly focused the Fed's energies on supporting the dollar on world exchanges and on keeping inflation down by means of a slightly higher discount rate. He has also endorsed repeal of certain regulations, dating from 1935, that separate the banking and securities industries, a position the White House shares. To this end, the Fed announced in January 1989 that banking companies would be allowed to raise money for corporations in the bond market, a function long performed only by securities brokers. Though the dollar and bank regulation are the Fed's main concerns, policy in the late 1980s may have more political content to it—the executive branch is working in closer concert with the Fed than it has since the 1950s in an effort to make the policies of the industrial nations' governments work. The Fed may be acting more independently of the Treasury department than it did in the 1930s and 1940s, but the Treasury's wishes and the Fed's wishes seem to be more in tandem than they were in the 1960s and 1970s. If the daily operations differ, the end result is nonetheless the same.

Such a two-pronged attack—the central bank working closely with its government—is understandable, given the nature of the world economy. The interests of the big industrial nations are very tightly intertwined, requiring more coordination of policy. New York and London are no longer the sole hubs of the financial world: There is a major stock, bond, and money market open somewhere on the globe around the clock, allowing every large financial institution to chase the cheapest loan or to find the highest rate of return for its money. And the central bank in most of the other major nations works much more closely with its government than the Fed does with the White House. Coordinating fiscal policy and monetary policy is crucial for every government in such a climate, and the Fed will increasingly be asked by the nation's political leaders to assist in this process. What some called "leaning against the wind" in the 1950s—contracting the money supply in the face of inflationary pressure, easing up when a slump seems near—still applies at the end of the 20th century. Now, however, it is wind of an international velocity, propelled by an integrated global economy, that the Fed must lean against.

Allowing for Opposition

Some economists remain critical of the Federal Reserve System. They argue that the system places too much power in the hands of administrators who are not elected. They complain that those administrators, because they need not run for election to their posts, could use their power in ways that would not benefit the general public. Others disagree with the philosophies of the administrators who run the Fed. Yet the need for a powerful and autonomous central bank was proven in the 19th century and again by the stock market crash of 1929. One story told by former member of the board of governors Nancy Teeters about herself may sum up the feeling in the economic community about the need for the Fed. Teeters, a Democrat, asked Chairman Arthur Burns, a Republican, if he was worried about her politics. Burns replied, "It doesn't matter, Nancy. In six months [here], everybody is a central banker."

As the Fed makes decisions based on its governors' philosophies, opponents will continue to criticize those decisions. Economics is a field that allows for many differences of opinion. With all its power, the Fed stands at the center of controversy whenever it takes action. Most observers predict that sooner or later politicians will find some reason to challenge the power of the Fed.

As long as the Fed continues to achieve its goals, however, it will be a strong institution. One important example of the Fed's success can be found in its actions following the stock market crash of October 19, 1987. On that date the nation's stock market suffered a loss of value just as severe as it suffered in 1929, and the crash of 1929 is generally cited as the event that touched off the

The Federal Reserve Bank of New York. As the site of all the system's open-market operations and of its foreign-exchange activities, the New York Fed is preeminent among the 12 district banks.

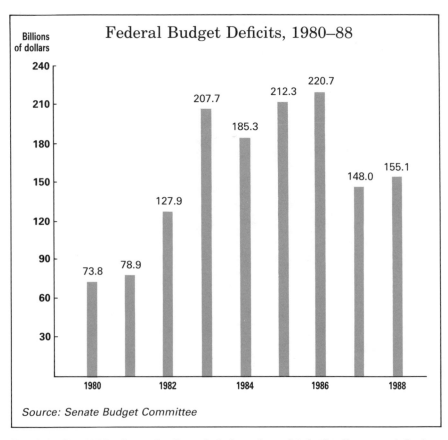

Billions of dollars

Federal Budget Deficits, 1980–88

240

220.7

210   212.3

207.7

185.3

180

155.1

150   148.0

127.9

120

90

78.9

73.8

60

30

1980   1982   1984   1986   1988

Source: Senate Budget Committee

During the 1980s, huge budget deficits—for which the Reagan Admin-istration and Congress blamed each other—made the Fed's job of up-holding the dollar's value far more difficult. Much of the shortfall was covered by foreign lenders, so the prospects for a strong dollar in the 1990s are shaky.

Great Depression. In 1987, however, the banking system remained strong. Businesses suffered no comparable level of failure.

In 1929 the Fed reacted to the market crash by tightening the money supply. Investors had already lost a large percentage of their savings when the value of their stock holdings fell. Unable to borrow more money to pay their debts, they suffered even more from the policies of the Fed. During the 1930s, Congress reacted to this by adding powers to the Federal Reserve Act, such as letting it place a ceiling on the amount of stock that could be bought on credit. The Fed also learned from past mistakes, responding to the crash of

94

1987 by loosening money and making it immediately available to borrowers. Banks were thus able to stand behind investment firms, and the stock market was stabilized. A total collapse was averted. Many economists later attributed the comparative stability to the Fed's actions.

Despite the criticisms and the philosophical disputes, it appears that the U.S. economy will always need the Fed to ensure stability and uphold the value of the dollar. A nation's currency can only be as strong as the government or individual making the promise to pay, and Americans rely on the Federal Reserve to keep the value of their money reasonably stable. As the international economy grows more interconnected and the dollar is used in more transactions around the world, other nations also depend on the Fed to maintain the dollar as a reliable medium of foreign exchange. Independent of many political pressures, the Fed can make the necessary decisions and force changes quickly when unexpected events threaten the nation's economy. Through times of crisis and contentment, the Fed will be operating behind the scenes of the banking industry to make sure money is a positive force in American society.

Organization of the
Federal Reserve System

FEDERAL ADVISORY COUNCIL
has 12 members

each is a prominent banker
elected by the directors
of each of the 12 F.R. Banks

BOARD OF GOVERNORS
has 7 members

each is appointed
by the president
and confirmed by the Senate

FEDERAL OPEN MARKET COMMITTEE (FOMC)
has 12 members:

the 7 governors;
the president of
the F.R. Bank of New York;
and the presidents
of 4 other F.R. Banks

12 FEDERAL RESERVE BANKS
(plus 25 branches
and 9 other offices
for processing checks)

Each bank has
9 directors:
3 bankers (called Class A);
3 business people (Class B);
and 3 others (Class C)

Together they appoint
a president,
a vice-president,
and other officers
and employees

MEMBER BANKS
about 5,400 banks
belong to the system
(or 2/5 of all U.S. banks)

Large: about 400
Medium: about 1,600
Small: about 3,400

Each group elects
one Class A and
one Class B director
to its F.R. Bank
(the Class C directors
are appointed by the
national board of governors)

GLOSSARY

Bank run   A crisis in which depositors lose confidence in the security of their bank and demand to withdraw their money, which has already been loaned to others.

Bond   An interest-bearing certificate of public or private indebtedness. The issuing agent (the borrower) must repay the amount of the bond by a specified date.

Central bank   A nonprofit bank administered by a national government for the purpose of funding its operations and, often, of acting as a stabilizing force on the nation's private banking industry.

Currency   A medium of exchange (coins, government-issued notes, bank notes) valid for general public circulation.

Deflation   A decrease in the volume of available money or credit, resulting in a decline of the general price level.

Discount rate   The rate of interest the Federal Reserve System charges on money it lends to banks in financial difficulty. By raising or lowering it, the Fed uses this rate to implement its monetary policy.

Elasticity   The degree of responsiveness to changes in the supply of or demand for cash and credit, as a result of changes in price or other variables.

Federal Funds rate   (or Interbank rate) The rate of interest one commercial bank charges another on overnight loans. Indirectly determined by the Fed, this rate generally stands a few percentage points higher than the discount rate.

Federal Reserve note   The sole legal tender (paper money) of the United States since 1928, when the last bank-issued notes were removed from circulation. The U.S. government guarantees each note's face value.

Fractional reserve   A method of banking in which only a portion of a customer's deposit is stored in a vault and the rest is transferred to someone else in the form of a loan.

Inflation An abnormal increase in available currency and credit beyond the proportion of available goods, resulting in a sharp and continuing rise in price levels.

Interest rate The price of loaned money. In a developed economy, the basic interest rate is set by the central bank to conform with the government's monetary policy. Private banks and other credit institutions charge higher rates to their customers in order to make a profit.

Keynesianism The theory that governments can increase the level of economic activity through deficit spending. Named for economist John Maynard Keynes, the practice gained credence during the Great Depression and has been widely used since.

Monetarism A theory holding that stable economic growth can be achieved only by a central bank's control of the rate of increase in the money supply.

Money supply The total amount of money in a nation's economy, including currency in circulation and various forms of bank deposits and credit.

Open-market operations The Fed's buying and selling of U.S. government securities, usually in large quantities, to alter the money supply.

Prime rate The interest rate that banks charge their most creditworthy customers. It stands a few percentage points higher than the Federal Funds rate.

Recession A period of reduced economic activity.

Securities Stock certificates or bonds that are evidence of property or debt.

Treasury note A bond or bill sold on the open market by the Federal Reserve, acting as agent for the U.S. Treasury, to finance the government's ongoing operations.

SELECTED REFERENCES

"America's Money Master," *Newsweek,* February 24, 1986.

Auerheimer, Leonardo, and Robert B. Ekelund. *The Essentials of Money and Banking.* New York: John Wiley, 1982.

Board of Governors, Federal Reserve System. *The Federal Reserve System: Purposes & Functions.* Washington, DC: Publications Services, Division of Support Services, Board of Governors of the Federal Reserve System, 1984.

Friedman, Milton, and Rose Friedman. *Free to Choose: A Personal Statement.* New York: Harcourt Brace Jovanovich, 1980.

Greider, William. *Secrets of the Temple: How the Federal Reserve Runs the Country.* New York: Simon & Schuster, 1988.

Groseclose, Elgin. *America's Money Machine: The Story of the Federal Reserve.* Westport, CT: Arlington House, 1980.

Heilbroner, Robert L., and Lester C. Thurow. *Economics Explained.* Englewood Cliffs, NJ: Prentice-Hall, 1982.

Johnson, Roger T. *Historical Beginnings . . . The Federal Reserve.* Boston: The Federal Reserve Bank of Boston, Banking and Public Services Division, 1982.

Kettl, Donald F. *Leadership at the Fed.* New Haven, CT: Yale University Press, 1986.

Little, Jeffrey B. *Wall Street—How It Works.* New York: Chelsea House, 1988.

Melton, William C. *Inside the Fed.* Homewood, IL: Dow Jones-Irwin, 1985.

Rothbard, Murray. *The Mystery of Banking.* New York: Richardson & Snyder, 1983.

Warfield, Gerald. *How to Read and Understand the Financial News.* New York: Harper & Row, 1986.

INDEX

Gary Taylor is the Houston correspondent for *Money* magazine, *The Journal of Commerce,* and *The National Law Journal.* He is a columnist for *Houston Metropolitan Magazine* and has written for *Time* magazine, the *New York Times,* and *USA Today.* Taylor was a reporter for the *Houston Post* for nine years and was nominated for a Pulitzer Prize in investigative journalism in 1977. He received a B.A. in journalism from the University of Missouri.

Arthur M. Schlesinger, jr., served in the White House as special assistant to Presidents Kennedy and Johnson. He is the author of numerous acclaimed works in American history and has twice been awarded the Pulitzer Prize. He taught history at Harvard College for many years and is currently Albert Schweitzer Professor of the Humanities at the City College of New York.

PICTURE CREDITS

AP/Wide World Photos: pp. 64, 65, 67, 71, 88, 90; Board of Governors, Federal Reserve System: pp. 50, 53, 56, 57, 60; The Carter Library: p. 68; Bruce Coleman: p. 14; Culver Pictures: pp. 23, 26, 40; Federal Reserve Bank of New York: cover (left), pp. 20, 93; Federal Reserve System: pp. 74, 81; Bill Fitzpatrick, The White House: p. 77; Debra P. Hershkowitz: cover (right); Library of Congress: pp. 25, 29, 30, 32, 34, 35, 37, 41, 42, 44, 45, 48, 53, 55, 63; National Archives: pp. 38, 46; *Newsweek:* p. 19; Donna Sinisgalli: p. 51; Peter Souza, The White House: p. 84; Gary Tong: pp. 73, 78, 94, 96; Harry S. Truman Library: p. 59; UPI/Bettmann Newsphotos: p. 86; U.S. Treasury Department: p. 16.

DATE DUE

11-30-90			

WGRL-HQ JUV
31057901803232
J 332.11 TAYLO
Taylor, Gary
The Federal Reserve System

HEADQUARTERS